The United Nations World Water Development Report 2014

FACING THE CHALLENGES

VOLUME 2

Published in 2014 by the United Nations Educational, Scientific and Cultural Organization, 7, place de Fontenoy, 75352 Paris 07 SP, France

© UNESCO 2014

Chapter 5, 'Infrastructure', © by International Bank for Reconstruction and Development/The World Bank.

ISBN 978-92-3-104259-1
ePub ISBN 978-92-3-904259-3

Suggested citation:
WWAP (United Nations World Water Assessment Programme). 2014. *The United Nations World Water Development Report 2014: Water and Energy*. Paris, UNESCO.

Cover and interior design and typesetting by Phoenix Design Aid A/S, an ISO 14001 (environmental management) and a DS 49001 (corporate social responsibility) certified and approved carbon neutral company.

Printed by UNESCO CLD, Paris.
This publication is printed with vegetable inks on FSC Mixed Sources paper, supporting responsible use of forest reserves. This is a carbon neutral print product. UNESCO Printing will contribute funds to a project replanting trees in Europe or Africa for this publication.
Printed in France

The United Nations World Water Development Report 2014 has been published on behalf of the United Nations World Water Assessment Programme by UNESCO with the support of the following organizations:

United Nations Funds and Programmes
United Nations Children's Fund (UNICEF)
United Nations Conference on Trade and Development (UNCTAD)
United Nations Department of Economic and Social Affairs (UNDESA)
United Nations Development Programme (UNDP)
United Nations Entity for Gender Equality and the Empowerment of Women (UN Women)
United Nations Environment Programme (UNEP)
United Nations High Commissioner for Refugees (UNHCR)
United Nations Human Rights Office of the High Commissioner (OHCHR)
United Nations Human Settlements Programme (UN-Habitat)
United Nations University (UNU)

Specialized United Nations Agencies
Food and Agriculture Organization of the United Nations (FAO)
International Atomic Energy Agency (IAEA)
International Bank for Reconstruction and Development (World Bank)
International Fund for Agricultural Development (IFAD)
International Labour Organization (ILO)
United Nations Educational, Scientific and Cultural Organization (UNESCO)
United Nations Industrial Development Organization (UNIDO)
United Nations Institute for Training and Research (UNITAR)
World Food Programme (WFP)
World Health Organization (WHO)
World Meteorological Organization (WMO)
World Tourism Organization (UNWTO)

United Nations Regional Commissions
Economic and Social Commission for Asia and the Pacific (UNESCAP)
Economic and Social Commission for Western Asia (UNESCWA)
Economic Commission for Africa (UNECA)
Economic Commission for Europe (UNECE)
Economic Commission for Latin America and the Caribbean (UNECLAC)

Secretariats of United Nations Conventions and Decades
Secretariat of the Convention to Combat Desertification (UNCCD)
Secretariat of the Convention on Biological Diversity (CBD)
Secretariat of the International Strategy for Disaster Reduction (UNISDR)
United Nations Framework Convention on Climate Change (UNFCCC)

Preparation of this report was made possible thanks to the financial support of the Italian Government.

TABLE OF CONTENTS

PREFACE

by Michela Miletto, WWAP Coordinator a.i.
and Engin Koncagül, WWDR 2014 Volume 2 Author

The fifth edition of the United Nations *World Water Development Report* (WWDR 2014) examines the close interdependency between water and energy, both of which are indispensable for the sustainable development of nations and the well-being of societies.

Despite their centrality to our lives, these two resources are not treated on an equal footing: while energy is considered as an important commercial industry, with great leverage due to market forces, freshwater is taken as public good, scaling relatively low in comparison to energy in broader policy circles. However, the need for energy in providing water services and the use of water in energy production form a critical nexus that requires a holistic approach by decision-makers. The common denominator in this difficult task is the alleviation of poverty: worldwide, the number of people whose right to water is not satisfied could be as high as 3.5 billion and more than 1.3 billion people still lack access to electricity, the lack of both of which are among the root causes of persistent human suffering.

Although little economic value is attributed to water resources, their irreplaceable role in the functioning of all sectors and in helping national economies to prosper is incontestable. In spite of ongoing efforts to improve water use efficiency, however, a business-as-usual approach has pushed the envelope beyond the limits of what is sustainable. And water demand will continue to grow in the foreseeable future, fuelled by population growth and consumption patterns that will simply add to the increasing competition for water resources, which the energy sector forms only one part of.

The WWDR 2014 concludes that the challenge for twenty-first century governance is to embrace the multiple aspects, roles and benefits of water, and to place water at the heart of decision-making in all water-dependent sectors. In particular, it calls for more coordinated planning between energy and water policies.

The thirteen case studies featured in this volume bolster the critical findings of the report by illustrating that an array of opportunities exists to exploit the benefits of synergies, such as energy recovery from sewerage water, the use of solar energy for wastewater treatment, and electricity production at 'drinking water power plants'. These examples also showcase alternatives to fossil fuel-based energy production, including hydropower development, geothermal energy, solar power and biogas.

Real-life examples clearly demonstrate that human creativity and an enabling environment – created by political guidelines that are adapted to national needs and realities – provide the right responses to these challenges.

The World Water Assessment Programme Secretariat is grateful to the country partners who contributed to the preparation of this volume by sharing their valuable experiences. We would like to invite others, too, to join us in forthcoming editions towards achieving global coverage. We are confident that you will find this compilation of case studies interesting and informative.

Michela Miletto

Engin Koncagül

*An investment in knowledge
pays the best interest*

Benjamin Franklin

PART 5 CASE STUDIES

Highlights of the findings

The fifth report in the United Nations *World Water Development Report* series (WWDR 2014) focuses on the close link between water and energy. As with previous reports, the in-depth treatment given to the subject in WWDR 2014 is accompanied by a volume of case studies, prepared by institutional and national partners who have assumed full ownership of this reporting process. The thirteen case studies (see map) presented in this volume provide real-life examples, from five regions, of responses to current water and energy challenges and imminent problems.

Regardless of the geographical setting or the level of national development, the overarching theme of the WWDR 2014 is highly relevant to all countries around the world, not only to the case study partners. Parallel to increasing living standards, the sustainability of escalating consumption of both water and energy resources has become a worldwide concern, with many national agendas recognizing the need to prioritize the decoupling of water use from energy generation. India, for example, has banned the construction of thermal power plants with open-loop wet cooling systems, which rely on high water consumption. As part of its national action plan on climate change, India has also targeted a 20% increase in water use efficiency in all sectors by 2017.

Fossil fuels remain the major source of energy worldwide, but renewable energy resources are gaining in popularity. Solar, geothermal, biogas, biochar and hydropower are just some of the technologies highlighted in this case study volume. Although the initial investments required to construct renewable energy generation facilities can be high, the long-term benefits of using environmentally friendly and sustainable methods to harness energy from natural processes – mostly with very low or zero carbon emission – can be advantageous.

Among the case studies featured, the ones from Mexico and the Gulf Cooperation Council (GCC) highlight the experimental use of solar energy for wastewater treatment and desalination. Desalination has become a necessity to meet increasing freshwater demand in the Gulf region. The energy intensive nature of this operation presents alarming projections: by 2035, Kuwait, for example, may have to allocate as much as 2.5 million barrels of oil per day for water desalination, equal to the country's entire 2011–2012 oil production. This business-as-usual scenario, to varying degrees, applies to other GCC countries. One notable response is the King Abdullah Initiative in Saudi Arabia, which has the ultimate goal of ensuring that all seawater desalination in the country will rely on solar energy alone by 2019.

Energy demands are rising across the globe and notably in developing countries, in parallel with industrialization, population growth and higher living standards. While fossil fuels continue to supply the biggest portion of this energy, mounting pollution and the financial burden of ever-increasing energy prices have spurred countries to reassess their use of energy resources. The case studies from Italy, Kenya and Turkey focus on geothermal energy, presenting different ways these countries have capitalized on this pollution-free resource, against a shared backdrop of increasing challenges in meeting national energy demands and achieving sustainable development without sacrificing the environment. For example, Turkey – an emerging market country and the world's seventeenth largest economy – spent US$60 billion on energy imports in 2012, a figure that seems likely to increase in coming years. Faced with this situation, the Turkish government introduced laws to incentivize development of renewable energy sources, especially the country's rich geothermal potential. With the participation of the private sector, Turkey's geothermal electricity production capacity doubled between 2009 and 2013. If fully utilized, geothermal resources can now meet 14% of Turkey's total energy needs. As well as the economic benefits, geothermal technologies offer many environmental advantages over conventional power. The Umbria region of Italy estimates that using geothermal heat to its full potential in its region alone would provide a reduction of more than four million tonnes of carbon dioxide emissions per year. In Kenya, geothermal energy is opted as a key response to overcome the country's energy bottleneck and to elevate its economy.

Hydropower is among the most common sources of renewable energy used today. This volume features three hydropower projects: the Three Gorges project in China, the Trebišnjica Multipurpose Hydrosystem in Bosnia and Herzegovina, and the Four Major Rivers Restoration project in the Republic of Korea. Together, these provide interesting examples of hydropower usage at very different scales. The Three Gorges Dam power station is the world's largest. In addition to generating electricity, the dam provides other advantages, including flood prevention, drought relief and improved inland water navigation. On a far more modest scale, the Four Major Rivers Restoration project in the Republic of Korea is the centrepiece and the most visible part of a larger national green growth strategy that prioritizes ecosystems and environmental sustainability. The Trebišnjica Multipurpose Hydrosystem in Eastern Herzegovina is designed to bring multiple benefits to a water scarce region that lies over a complex karst system.

One of the two case studies from Japan also highlights the versatility of dams, by illustrating how hydropower stations bridged the gap in electricity generation following the shutdown of numerous nuclear and thermal power stations in the aftermath of the Great East Japan Earthquake in 2011.

Wastewater is commonly discharged into rivers, lakes or seas with little (if any) treatment, but the case studies from Austria and Japan highlight innovative ways to harness the potential of waste and turn it into a rich energy source. Gasification in Tokyo, biochar production in Hiroshima, the use of biogas in Kobe and the development of energy self-sufficient wastewater treatment plants in Vienna are good examples of ways that technology can contribute to making our societies more sustainable.

The drinking water power plants in and around Vienna demonstrate some of the potential of resource conservation, which in this case provides the dual benefits of generating renewable energy while reducing water pressure, which is essential for the longevity of the water supply infrastructure.

The case study from Austin, Texas, USA, is a good example of productive collaboration between public water and electricity utilities to identify and exploit synergies and develop integrated programmes and policies. Through research and pilot projects, the city is exploring better and more sustainable uses of both its water and its energy resources. This fruitful cooperation has allowed both utilities to increase their supply capacity in a controlled fashion without the need for major expansion efforts.

Clearly, in spite of growing efforts, water is yet to be decoupled from the complex energy equation. Nevertheless the case studies presented in this volume illustrate some of the options currently available to reduce this looming water and energy crisis. The handful of examples provided remind us, moreover, of the stark truth that the full value of water is still unrecognized, and that there is much room for improvement if we are to curb the unsustainable business-as-usual approaches that have brought us to the situation we find ourselves in today. That said, these positive and often ingenious developments also give us reason to remain cautiously optimistic. It is our heartfelt belief that building the momentum in such initiatives will bring incommensurate rewards: environmental sustainability and poverty alleviation at the global level.

Regional distribution of the case studies

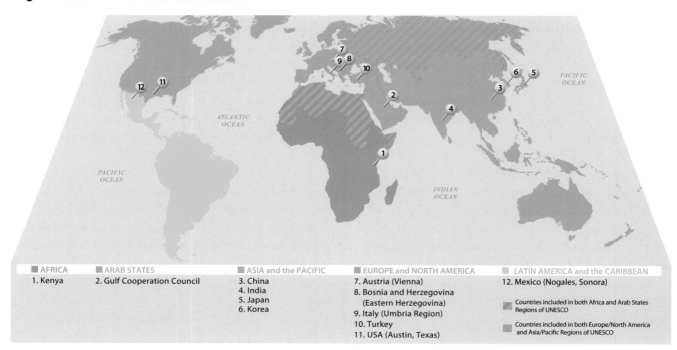

AFRICA	ARAB STATES	ASIA and the PACIFIC	EUROPE and NORTH AMERICA	LATIN AMERICA and the CARIBBEAN
1. Kenya	2. Gulf Cooperation Council	3. China 4. India 5. Japan 6. Korea	7. Austria (Vienna) 8. Bosnia and Herzegovina (Eastern Herzegovina) 9. Italy (Umbria Region) 10. Turkey 11. USA (Austin, Texas)	12. Mexico (Nogales, Sonora) Countries included in both Africa and Arab States Regions of UNESCO Countries included in both Europe/North America and Asia/Pacific Regions of UNESCO

17 Green energy generation in Vienna, Austria

Vienna's drinking water comes from mountain springs through two long-distance pipelines. The elevation drop allows the gravity flow to turn turbines installed within what are commonly referred to as drinking water power plants (DWPPs), which generate electricity while reducing the water pressure to levels suitable for the city's drinking water infrastructure. This provides the energy necessary to operate the system itself, as well as surplus electricity which is then sold to utility companies.

The use of such energy-generating systems was temporarily suspended in the 1970s due to economic considerations mainly arising from stagnant energy prices. New pipes with valves to control water pressure were installed to bypass the turbines. In the mid-1990s, however, electricity prices recovered and renewable energy resources became increasingly sought in Austria. This led to the re-operationalization of Vienna's abandoned water turbines and the construction of new plants.

The DWPP at Mauer, along the Second Mountain Spring Pipeline, was the first new plant to be constructed, while the older DWPP at Reithof, located along the First Mountain Spring Pipeline, was upgraded to boost its initial capacity of 45 kW (in 1929) to 340 kW. The turbines neither alter water quality nor block water flow to jeopardize reliable water supply.

By 2011, more than 65 million kWh electricity was being generated annually by 14 such plants located within and around the city of Vienna, contributing towards achieving the European Community target of a 20% share of energy from renewable sources by 2020 (Directive 2009/28/EC). The city is actively seeking further potential sites for such plants, as well as drawing

---

BOX 17.1

An energy self-sufficient wastewater treatment plant

Ebswien, Vienna's main wastewater treatment plant, purifies approximately 220 million m³ sewage per year. The power used by the plant accounts for almost 1% of the city's total electricity consumption. Confronted by rising energy costs, however, city officials have turned to innovative approaches to reduce Ebswien's energy consumption.

The plant uses a number of renewable energy technologies, such as hydropower, solar energy (thermal and photovoltaic), wind power and methane, to lessen dependency on carbon-based energy sources and to decrease greenhouse gas emissions.

These technologies have been carefully implemented to function in an integrated manner. A turbine installed at the point of discharge, where the treated effluent is drained into the Danube River, generates approximately 1.5 GWh electricity annually. Solar thermal and photovoltaic power units are also built into the compound, and a small wind turbine generates sufficient current to power the exterior lighting. An integrated block heat and power station utilizes approximately 20 million m³ methane that has been recovered during the treatment process, producing 78 GWh electricity and 82 GWh heat output per year. In addition, the plant's energy consumption has been reduced significantly through process optimization and infrastructural measures such as using energy saving bulbs and efficient heating technologies.

As a result of these combined technologies, the Ebswien wastewater treatment plant is not only energy self-sufficient until 2020, but also produces a surplus of approximately 15 GWh electricity and 42 GWh heat output annually. The reduction in greenhouse gas emissions is estimated at approximately 40,000 tonnes per year, equivalent to that of a town of 4,000 inhabitants.

Source: Adapted from Ebswien hauptkläranlage (n.d.) and Umwelttecnik.at (2012).

on other renewable energy technologies to boost its green energy generation potential (Box 17.1).

Conclusion

Vienna features a number of innovative green energy approaches. The city's many DWPPs are prime examples of resource conservation, providing the dual benefits of renewable energy generation and water pressure reduction (which also enhances the longevity of water supply infrastructure). In addition, the Ebswien wastewater treatment plant incorporates various renewable energy technologies to generate more than sufficient energy to power the plant. This highlights an energy-aware approach to wastewater management.

The two projects featured in this case study result in a reduction in carbon dioxide emissions of tens of thousands of tonnes per year when compared to the generation of electricity through carbon-based energy sources. Environmental protection, cost efficiency and curbing climate change are all valuable advantages of these approaches.

References

Except where other sources are cited, information in this chapter is adapted from:

European Commission. n.d. *Renewable Energy*. Brussels, European Commission. http://ec.europa.eu/energy/renewables/targets_en.htm (Accessed Jul 2013)

Vienna Water. n.d. *Generating Energy with Drinking Water: The Mauer Small-Scale Hydropower Plant*. Vienna, Vienna City Administration. http://www.wien.gv.at/english/environment/watersupply/energy.html (Accessed Jul 2013)

****

Ebswien hauptkläranlage. n.d. *EOS: Energie-Optimierung Schlammbehandlung*. Vienna, Ebswien hauptkläranlage GmbH. http://www.ebswien.at/hauptklaeranlage/hauptklaeranlage/abwasser-energie/projekt-eos/ (Accessed Sep 2013)

Umwelttecnik.at. 2012. *Main Wastewater Treatment Plant in Vienna Becomes Energy-Self-Sufficient*. Vienna, Green Jobs Austria. http://www.umwelttechnik.at/en/water-and-wastewater/wastewater-management/good-practise/main-waste-water-treatment-plant-in-vienna-becomes-energy-self-sufficient/

The Yangtze River originates in the Qinghai–Tibetan Plateau and runs from west to east through 11 provinces. With its main stream extending more than 6,300 km, it is the longest river in China and the third longest in the world. Its basin area covers about 20% of China's landmass and holds more than one-third of the country's population (Figure 18.1). Economic activities in the basin generate nearly 40% of Gross Domestic Product.

The Three Gorges project was designed to tame the Yangtze River, which floods frequently and severely. The project commenced in 1993 and was completed in 2010. The project's main structure is the 181 m high Three Gorges Dam. It not only regulates the river's flow, but also is used to generate electricity and for water navigation. The dam is well known for its hydroelectric power station, which is the world's biggest in terms of installed capacity.

The dam reservoir stores approximately 39.3 billion m³ water and covers an area of 1,084 km². The Three Gorges' reservoir, which includes a number of ship locks and

a ship lift, improved water navigability over a 660 km stretch of the Yangtze River (Box 18.1).

Before the Three Gorges project, droughts and floods frequently affected the Yangtze River basin. According to records, on average, each province in the basin suffered from flood disaster every ten years and from drought every two to three years. The most recent example is the 2011 drought in the lower Yangtze River, which corresponded to the severity of a 100-year frequency drought. To offset the severely reduced natural water flow, about 5.5 billion m³ water was released from the dam reservoir, mainly for irrigation and municipal use. This reduced the effects of the drought, ensuring navigation safety and meeting environmental requirements.

In central and eastern China, periodic floods cause considerable economic losses. The Three Gorges project has significantly enhanced the flood control capability in the middle and lower reaches of the Yangtze River. Between 2003 and 2012, a total of 75 billion m³ floodwater

The Yangtze River basin

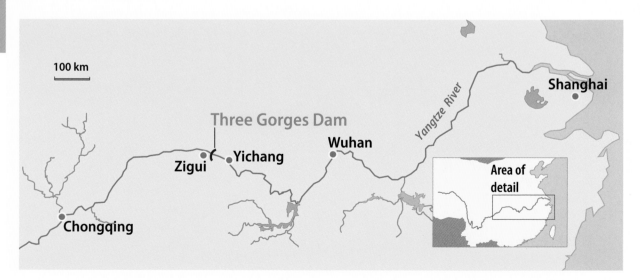

was controlled and stored in the dam reservoir. Of this, approximately 27 billion m³ was stored during the 2010 floods.

The project has also allowed easy and permanent access by boat to the beautiful scenery along the Yangtze River. The dam itself, the hydroelectric power station and the ship locks are new man-made attractions that draw tourists from all over the world. In 2012, 1.8 million tourists visited the area. A stretch of the Yangtze River that flows through deep gorges in western Yunnan is a UNESCO World Heritage site.

The highlight of the project is its large installed capacity for hydroelectric power production, which provides electricity to eastern, southern and central China – where power shortages used to be a severe problem. Thirty-four generating units with a total installed capacity of 22,500 MW make the hydroelectric power station in the Three Gorges dam the world's biggest. Its daily power production accounts for 2% of China's total. From 2003, when the dam started operation up to 2012, a total of 630 billion kWh electricity was generated. In 2012, electricity production reached 98.1 billion kWh, equivalent to 14% of the country's total hydroelectric power output. At this rate, the annual electric power generation is equivalent to several large-scale thermal power stations, consuming as much as 50 million tonnes of coal per year. From this perspective, the Three Gorges

hydroelectric power station could reduce annual carbon dioxide emissions by up to 100 million tonnes. Its strategic location and great capacity have made it the main hub of the national power grid. The hydroelectric power generated at the Three Gorges brings direct benefits to more than half of China's population.

Even though a great deal of preparation and planning went into the project's preliminary phase, it has brought about changes in the area's social and environmental fabric. In 2011, China's State Council acknowledged that 'the project has provided great benefits in terms of flood prevention, power generation, river transportation and water resource utilization, but it has also brought about some urgent problems in terms of environmental protection, the prevention of geological hazards and the welfare of relocated communities' (Central People's Government of the People's Republic of China, 2013). The Chinese government pledged to establish disaster warning systems, reinforce riverbanks, boost funding for environmental protection and improve benefits for the resettled communities (Hays, 2011).

Conclusion

The Three Gorges project is a multipurpose water resources development scheme. The actual investment in the construction and the resettlement amounted to approximately US$29 billion. However, this cost will be rapidly paid off through the cumulative benefits

---

18.1 BOX

Navigation on the Yangtze River

Also known as 'the golden waterway', the Yangtze River has been used by boats for centuries, especially along the middle and lower reaches of the river's main stream. However, before the construction of the Gezhouba and Three Gorges dams, some sections were only navigable seasonally. This hindered the economic development of the western region because it limited trade between the south-west and the more developed eastern regions of the country.

Located in the Xiling Gorge, one of the Three Gorges of the Yangtze River, the Three Gorges dam improves waterway conditions from Yichang as far west as Chongqing City. As a result, ships from inland ports are now able to transport goods all the way to the sea at Shanghai. The navigational infrastructure, established as part of the project, includes double-way, five-tier ship locks with the highest water head and the most steps in the world. The total length of the ship locks' main structure is 1,607 m and it can accommodate barge fleets weighing up to 10,000 tonnes. In 2011, the cargo that passed through the ship locks reached 100 million tonnes for the first time – which is six times the cargo weight of 2003. Overall, from June 2003 to the end of 2011, over half a billion tonnes of cargo was transported through the ship locks, providing a huge boost to the economic development of China's western and middle-eastern regions. The navigation industry alone created 150,000 jobs in the Chongqing area. Other navigation-related activities created more than 500,000 jobs. All in all, over two million people have been employed.

The lower cost of transporting boats has helped to reduce fuel consumption and greenhouse gas emissions substantially. In 2009 for example, 500,000 tonnes of fuel was saved thanks to water transport departing from Chongqing City. This, in practical terms, translates into a reduction of 1.5 million tonnes of carbon dioxide emissions.

obtained, notably in minimizing the impact of floods and droughts. To give an example, the economic damage caused by the 1998 flood in the Yangtze River basin was practically equal to the total investment in the Three Gorges project. Other dimensions, such as electricity generation and river navigation, make the project even more cost-efficient. The revenue generated by electricity sales alone is expected to cover the investment by 2015. The production of hydroelectricity and improvements in river transport also contributed to significant reductions in greenhouse gas emissions. The project's role in regulating flow has improved water quality in the river during drought periods through dilution. However, the Three Gorges project has also caused new environmental problems: the inundation of arable lands and rare plants; weakened self-purification capacity in certain tributary sections of the river basin; and changed aquatic ecosystems in the reservoir area, as well as in the middle and lower reaches of the Yangtze River. These and other emerging problems have been acknowledged by the Chinese government, which has pledged to take improvement measures.

Acknowledgement

Three Gorges Corporation

References

Except where other sources are cited, information in this chapter is adapted from:

China Three Gorges Corporation. 2013. *Three Gorges Project Case Study.* Beijing, China Three Gorges Corporation. (Unpublished)

****

Central People's Government of the People's Republic of China. 2013. [*The State Council Adopted the Three Gorges Follow-up Plan.*] http://www.gov.cn/ldhd/2011-05/18/content_1866289.htm (In Chinese)

Hays, J. 2011. *Three Gorges Dam: Benefits, Problems and Costs. Facts and Details.* http://factsanddetails.com/china/cat13/sub85/item1046.html

Hydropower development in Eastern Herzegovina: The Trebišnjica Multipurpose Hydrosystem

Eastern Herzegovina is a region of some 7,500 km² in the south-eastern part of Bosnia and Herzegovina. For the purposes of this case study, it refers to the area delineated by the Neretva River in the west, Montenegro in the east and Croatia in the south-west. In spite of abundant rainfall that ranges from 1,250 mm to about 2,450 mm per year, access to water is a challenge as a result of the karst terrain which allows almost 80% of rainwater to immediately percolate deep into the ground, making permanent surface flow rare. Four of the five rivers in Eastern Herzegovina (the Trebišnjica, Zalomka, Bregava, Mušnica and Buna rivers) disappear into complex underground structures within relatively short distances of their sources and reappear as permanent or temporary springs in various locations (Figure 19.1). Water availability becomes an even more pressing issue during dry summer periods when demands for domestic use and irrigation are highest. In remote areas, villagers rely on rainwater collected during winter and groundwater from siphonal lakes in natural karst shafts. The region's only agricultural land is in the karst *poljes* – flat-floored

geographic depressions which, under natural conditions, remain flooded for between 150 and 250 days per year. With an estimated 100,000 inhabitants living in the region in 2006, the population of Eastern Herzegovina remains low. Difficult living conditions have been driving people out of this region over many decades.

In contrast to the limited surface water resources in Eastern Herzegovina, there is a considerable amount of groundwater available in the region. However, this has not been sufficiently investigated. This is why the economic and social development of the region currently depends on being able to optimize the use of its scarce surface water resources. Among these, the Trebišnjica River is the most important; it is the longest sinking river in Europe with a total length of 90 km, of which about 30 km is permanent. The Trebišnjica Multipurpose Hydrosystem (TMH) aims to harness the potential energy of this river. The project, which was initiated in 1959, consists of seven dams, six artificial reservoirs, six tunnels and four channels (see also Box 19.1). Producing

<table>
<tr><td>19.1
FIGURE</td><td>**Groundwater flow directions in Eastern Herzegovina including the border areas of Montenegro and Croatia**</td></tr>
</table>

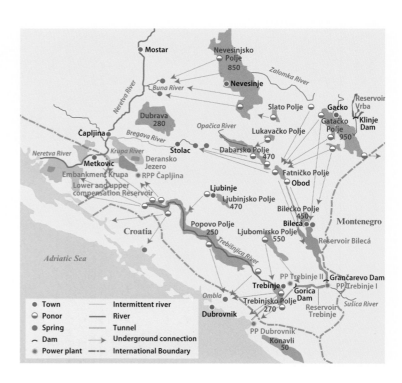

Note: Ponor is a natural surface opening that may be found in karstic areas.
Source: Adapted from DIKTAS (2011).

hydropower is the main priority of the TMH because exporting electricity to neighbouring countries is Eastern Herzegovina's main source of income. However, the project also aims to provide water for all sectors, including for fish farming, for recreational purposes and for the prevention of deforestation.

The TMH has not been fully implemented yet and only the lower part – from sea level up to an elevation of 400 m – is in operation. Four dams (Table 19.1) in this section have, between them, an installed capacity of 818 MW, enabling them to generate around 2,700 GWh electricity per year. The finalization of the upper part of

TABLE 19.1

Technical characteristics of water reservoirs and power plants on the lower section of the Trebišnjica Multipurpose Hydrosystem (TMH)

Hydropower plant	Reservoir capacity (million m³)	Installed capacity (MW)	Average annual electricity generation (GWh)
Trebinje I	1 280.0	180	571
Trebinje II	15.9	8	22
Dubrovnik	–*	210	1 564
Čapljina	5.2	420	620

Note: * Dubrovnik does not have reservoir capacity as the water for hydropower production flows via a tunnel from the reservoir of Trebinje II.

BOX 19.1

The Dinaric Karst and the DIKTAS project

The Dinaric Karst covers a large area extending from Italy to Greece. Highly porous rock formations in this system serve as conduits that allow groundwater to cover long distances. Eastern Herzegovina, including the Trebišnjica River basin, is a part of this extensive karst formation.

The main water-related challenge in Eastern Herzegovina is to deal with the regularly alternating summer droughts and winter and spring floods. One of the aims of the Trebišnjica Multipurpose Hydrosystem (TMH) is to minimize this challenge, while providing other benefits to the residents of the region. Four hydropower plants (Table 19.1) were built between 1954 and 1981 as a part of the lower section of the project (Figure 19.1). These power plants are currently situated in two countries, Croatia, and Bosnia and Herzegovina, which formed following the break-up of Yugoslavia in the early 1990s. The technical challenges of water resources development in a complex karst system were further compounded by the political difficulties that set in in the aftermath of the civil war that broke out in 1992. Consequently, the realization of the upper section of TMH has been slowed down substantially as a result of limited cooperation among political entities in Bosnia and Herzegovina as well as among neighbouring countries.

Similar challenges are present in the broader setting of the Dinaric Karst, as it is the major source of freshwater for Croatia, Bosnia and Herzegovina, Montenegro and Albania. The Global Environment Facility (GEF) funded the Protection and Sustainable Use of the Dinaric Karst Aquifer System (DIKTAS) project, which is a pioneering effort that aims to introduce sustainable integrated water resources management principles in such an extensive transboundary karst aquifer system. DIKTAS is implemented by UNEP and executed by UNESCO's International Hydrological Programme. The core DIKTAS project partners – Albania, Bosnia and Herzegovina, Croatia and Montenegro – agreed to create two mechanisms to facilitate enhanced consultation and the exchange of information between the government entities that are involved in water resources management: national inter-ministerial committees (NICs) in each of the project countries and a consultation and information exchange (CIE) body at the regional level. The NICs and CIE together represent the key combination of technical and political experts involved in the project who will discuss, comment and approve the project's products, such as transboundary diagnostic analysis (TDA), environmental quality objectives, and environmental status indicators and their long-term monitoring. The NICs and CIE will have a central role in the preparation and implementation of the Strategic Action Programme aimed at harmonizing existing policy and institutional frameworks.

Source: Adapted from DIKTAS (2013).

the TMH at elevations between 400 m and 1,000 m above sea level has been pending for years, delayed as a result of the civil war. Hydropower plants due to be built at Nevesinje, Dabar and Bileća in the highlands will, when they come online, boost power capacity by almost 250 MW and augment the benefits that the TMH has already brought to the people of the region. Prevailing political stability and growing cooperation will certainly facilitate the construction of these plants resuming without a long delay.

Unconventional structures such as underground dams and water collecting galleries are being considered to make the best use of underground water resources, which so far have not been tapped. One such technically challenging project in the region is the Ombla underground dam near Dubrovnik in Croatia, which is currently under consideration for construction. The Ombla River rises as a karst spring and is fed by groundwater that is partly replenished by the Trebišnjica River.

Conclusion

Temporarily flooded karst *poljes*, ephemeral rivers, numerous caves and deep underground flows characterize the terrain of Eastern Herzegovina. In spite of abundant rainfall, karst terrain and the uneven distribution of precipitation makes its inhabitants vulnerable to frequent floods and droughts. The TMH was initiated in the early 1950s to improve the livelihoods of the people in the region by regulating water supply to make it available all year round for

multiple uses, most notably electricity generation. The hydropower plants that were built as a part of the TMH are the most important agents of economic development in Eastern Herzegovina. However, the complex karstic system and the state borders that dissect the region make the integrated management of water resources complex. In the face of increasing demand for water and energy, optimizing the use of water resources using a holistic approach calls for a common effort to be made by all stakeholders in the region. In this context, DIKTAS is a noteworthy project that contributes to the process of building a bridge of cooperation between political entities and countries in the Dinaric Karst region.

Acknowledgements
Petar Milanović, Neno Kukurić

References
Except where other sources are cited, information in this chapter summary is adapted from:

Milanović, P. and Kukurić, N. 2013. *Hydropower and Groundwater in Karst*. Delft, the Netherlands, International Groundwater Resources Assessment Centre (IGRAC). http://www.un-igrac.org/publications/478

****

DIKTAS (Protection and Sustainable Use of the Dinaric Karst Aquifer System). 2011. *Waters of the Trebišnjica River* (brochure). DIKTAS.

––––. 2013. Project Website. DIKTAS. http://diktas.iwlearn.org/ (Accessed Sep 2013)

Water and energy are crucial for development. The Gulf Cooperation Council (GCC) countries (Saudi Arabia, Qatar, United Arab Emirates, Oman, Bahrain and Kuwait), situated in one of the most water scarce regions of the world, are facing a critical challenge in addressing growing interdependency between these two resources. Without energy, mainly in the form of electricity, water cannot be delivered for its multiple uses. Water is also needed for energy production, notably for cooling and enhanced oil recovery processes in the region, in addition to other applications.

The population of the GCC countries is almost 45 million (Markaz, 2012), and is projected to reach 70 million by 2050. This demographic growth, along with accelerated socio-economic development, has led to a substantial increase in water demand, placing further stress on scarce and mainly non-renewable water resources in the region. Growing water demand has also necessitated the use of more energy for the provision of water supply. It is estimated that water services currently account

for at least 15% of national electricity consumption in most of the Arab countries. This share is continuously on the rise (Khatib, 2010). Intergovernmental Panel on Climate Change (IPCC) assessments show that the limited amount of water that is available in the region is expected to further decline as a result of climate change and human-induced quality problems (Bates et al., 2008). Consequently, more energy will be required to treat poor quality water for drinking and food production, or to pump water from greater depths or transfer it from greater distances. The main concern linked to growing water–energy interdependency is the increasing greenhouse gas emissions which, based on current trends, are expected to double to 9% of global emissions by 2035 (Khatib, 2010). In other words, climate change is expected to increase both water and energy needs, thus creating a feedback loop of environmental deterioration.

Given the region's limited endowment of renewable water resources, desalination, mainly through cogeneration power desalting plants (CPDPs), has become a common but energy intensive method of satisfying the increasing demand for water. In fact, about 50% of the world's desalination capacity is installed in the GCC countries (Dawoud and Al Mulla, 2012), and combined annual capacity in the region is projected to reach 19 billion m³ by as early as 2016 (GWI, 2010) (Figure 20.1). In 2005, the average share of desalinated water destined for municipal use in the GCC countries was around 55% (World Bank and AGFUND, 2005). This ratio is expected to increase gradually because of the ongoing deterioration of the quality of the groundwater.

Although GCC countries are rich in fossil fuels, meeting escalating demand for water by expanding desalination has become a very hydrocarbon intensive process, claiming a sizeable portion of the main export of these countries. For example, in Saudi Arabia, which has more than 18% of the world's desalination capacity, 25% of domestic oil and gas production is used to produce water through CPDPs. If the current trend continues, this share

FIGURE

Current (2010) and contracted (2016) desalination capacity in the Gulf Cooperation Council countries

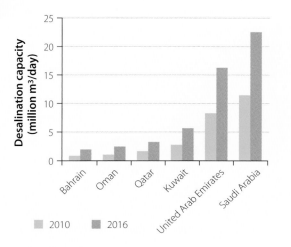

Source: GWI (2010).

will reach as high as 50% by 2030 (Al-Hussayen, 2009). Similarly, in Kuwait electricity and desalinated water consumption have been on the rise – practically doubling every decade as a result of population growth and the rise in living standards. Projections show that in a business-as-usual scenario, the energy demand of desalination plants will be equal to the country's 2011–2012 oil production (2.5 million barrels of oil per day) by the year 2035 (Darwish et al., 2009).

Undoubtedly, these projections are alarming both from a sustainability point of view as well as in the light of environmental concerns such as greenhouse gas emissions and seawater pollution by discharged brines, a by-product of desalination (Abderrahman and Hussain, 2006). While the impact of discharges from thermal desalination plants has not been studied in depth at the regional level, given the enclosed nature of the Gulf, the GCC countries are increasingly concerned by the potential damage to the fragile marine ecosystem (Al-Jamal and Schiffler, 2009). In general, the information that is currently available indicates that there is a need for a comprehensive environmental evaluation of all major desalination projects at the global level (Lattemann and Höpner, 2003). From the sustainable development aspect of coastal areas, the integration of desalination activities into regional water resources management plans is an important consideration (UNEP-MAP/MED POL, 2003).

Using solar energy as a vast renewable resource in the region is being considered as a way of decoupling expanding desalination projects' dependence on hydrocarbon energy sources (Box 20.1). The use of other potential energy sources, such as biogas (methane) that has been recovered from wastewater treatment plants, is one of the viable solutions to reducing the environmental footprint of producing more energy to keep pace with rising demands for water provision and services.

The GCC countries have recognized that good water management is just as important as technical solutions are in trying to ease water scarcity. In their thirty-first summit in 2010, the GCC heads of state issued the Abu Dhabi Declaration, which acknowledged the strong link between water and energy. The Declaration, among other matters, called for a comprehensive long-term strategy for water resources in the GCC countries that would take into account the interdependencies between water, energy and agriculture, the effects of climate change, and the environmental impact of desalination, emphasizing water demand management and conservation. The Declaration consisted of many recommendations on using water and energy efficiently, including the use of economic, technological, legislative and societal awareness tools. Most importantly, the Declaration linked water security with energy security and considered both as crucial strategic priorities for the future of the GCC countries.

Conclusion

Addressing water scarcity is considered a major challenge in the GCC countries, which are situated in one of the most water-stressed regions of the world. These countries have so far been able to alleviate the challenge by tapping fossil groundwater resources and using seawater desalination as a complementary source. However, an increase in the amount of water being used has led to the depletion of some aquifers and a deterioration of quality in others. This has made desalination necessary to meet various water demands, notably municipal uses. In 2005, desalinated water accounted for more than half of the drinking water supply in the GCC countries and

---

20.1 BOX

The King Abdullah Initiative for Solar Water Desalination

In the Gulf Cooperation Council (GCC) region, there are a number of initiatives related to the water–energy nexus. Probably one of the most important on the supply side is the King Abdullah Initiative for Solar Water Desalination, which was launched in 2010. The initiative aims to use solar energy to desalinate seawater at a low cost to contribute to Saudi Arabia's water security and the national economy (Al Saud, 2010). The implementation of the initiative will be done in three stages over nine years. The first phase, which will last three years, aims to build a desalination plant with a production capacity of 30,000 m³/day to meet the drinking water needs of the town of Al Khafji. The plant will use reverse osmosis technology and will be powered by solar energy farms that are currently being constructed. The second phase aims to build another solar desalination plant with a production capacity of 300,000 m³/day. The third phase would involve the construction of several solar plants for desalination in all parts of the country. The ultimate goal is to enable all seawater desalination in the country to be carried out using solely solar energy by 2019, and at a significantly lower cost of US$0.4/m³ compared to the current cost of between US$0.67/m³ and US$1.47/m³ when using thermal methods. The technology developed here would also be licensed outside Saudi Arabia (Sustainable Energy, 2010).

this ratio is expected to grow. The total installed capacity of desalination plants in the region has reached almost half of worldwide production at the expense of intensive fossil fuel use as the main source of energy. However, environmental impacts, such as greenhouse gas emissions and the by-products of desalination require careful consideration to be able to achieve water security without sacrificing the environment. Projects aimed at using alternative and renewable energy sources such as solar, wind and biogas from wastewater can help to decouple carbon intensive energy production and the growing need for water desalination. The importance of integrated management approaches to water and energy resources as well as conservation efforts have been recognized by all countries at the highest level.

Acknowledgement

Waleed K. Al-Zubari

References

Except where other sources are cited, information in this chapter is adapted from:

Al-Zubari, W.K. 2013. *The Water Energy Nexus in the GCC Countries.* Bahrain, Water Resources Management Program, College of Graduate Studies, Arabian Gulf University. (Unpublished)

****

Abderrahman, W. and Hussain, T. 2006. Pollution impacts of desalination on ecosystems in the Arabian Peninsula. Amer, K.M. et al. (eds), *Policy Perspectives for Ecosystem and Water Management in the Arabian Peninsula.* Paris/Hamilton, Canada, UNESCO/UNU-INWEH. http://www.unesco.org/ulis/cgi-bin/ulis.pl?catno=150698&set=529F1AF4_0_476&gp=1&lin=1&ll=1

Bates, B., Kundzewicz, Z.W., Wu, S. and Palutikof, J. 2008. *Climate Change and Water.* Technical Paper of the Intergovernmental Panel on Climate Change (IPCC). Geneva, IPCC. http://www.ipcc.ch/pdf/technical-papers/climate-change-water-en.pdf

Darwish, M.A., Al-Najem, N.M. and Lior, N. 2009. Towards sustainable seawater desalting in the Gulf area. *Desalination,* 235(1–3): 58–87.

Dawoud, A.M. and Al Mulla, M.M. 2012. Environmental impacts of seawater desalination: Arabian Gulf case study. *International Journal of Environment and Sustainability,* 1(3): 22–37.

GWI (Global Water Intelligence). 2010. *Desalination Markets 2010: Global Forecast and Analysis.* Oxford, UK, GWI.

Al-Hussayen, A. 2009. Inaugural speech by the Minister of Water and Electricity, Saudi Arabia. Jeddah, Saudi Water and Power Forum.

Al-Jamal, K. and Schiffler, M. 2009. Desalination opportunities and challenges in the Middle East and North Africa region. N. V. Jagannathan et al. (eds), *Water in the Arab World: Management Perspectives and Innovations,* pp. 479–494. Washington DC, World Bank.

Khatib, H. 2010. The water and energy nexus in the Arab region. *Arab Water Report: Towards Improved Water Governance.* Nairobi, UNDP. (Unpublished)

Lattemann, S. and Höpner T. 2003. *Seawater Desalination: Impacts of Brine and Chemical Discharges on the Marine Environment.* L'Aquila, Italy, Balaban Desalination Publications.

Markaz (Kuwait Financial Centre). 2012. *GCC Demographic Shift: Intergenerational Risk-Transfer at Play.* Kuwait, Markaz. http://www.markaz.com/DesktopModules/CRD/Attachments/DemographicsResearch-MarkazResearch-June%202012.pdf

Al Saud, T.M. 2010. *King Abdullah Initiative for Solar Water Desalination.* Presentation at the Saudi International Water Technology Conference, Riyadh, Saudi Arabia, 21 November 2011. http://kacstwatertech.org/eng/presentatoins/Day1/Session_1_1/Turki.pdf

Sustainable Energy. 2010. Regional news and trends: Saudi Arabia. *Sustainable Energy,* 1(3): 25. Nicosia, Middle East Economic Survey (MEES). http://www.mees.com/system/assets/000/000/628/original_issue3.pdf

UNEP-MAP/MED POL. 2003. *Sea Water Desalination in the Mediterranean: Assessment and Guidelines.* MAP Technical Reports Series No. 139. Athens, United Nations Environment Programme (UNEP)-Mediterranean Action Plan (MAP). http://195.97.36.231/acrobatfiles/MTSAcrobatfiles/mts139eng.pdf

World Bank and AGFUND. 2005. *A Water Sector Assessment Report on the Countries of the Cooperation Council of the Arab States of the Gulf.* World Bank Report No. 32539-M. Washington DC, World Bank. https://openknowledge.worldbank.org/bitstream/handle/10986/8719/325390ENGLISH01eport0Clean006125105.pdf?sequence=1

21 | Water use efficiency in thermal power plants in India

With more than 1.2 billion people, India is the second most populous country in the world – and according to estimates, it will be the most crowded nation by 2025. In parallel to its rapid population growth and increase of water consumption in all sectors, the country's per capita water availability declined threefold over the past six decades (from over 5,000 m^3 in 1951 to 1,600 m^3 in 2011). Agriculture, which accounts for 85% of all water use, continues to be the national priority. Taking these factors into consideration, the combined demand for water is likely to reach or outstrip availability by 2050. This alarming projection calls for water to be mainstreamed in all planning activities nationwide.

A sustainable supply of energy is vital if India is to keep its momentum as one of the fastest growing major economies in the world. In fact, the country is the fifth largest electricity producer at the global level. And yet more than half the population lacks access to electricity, and India's per capita electricity consumption is less than one-quarter of the world average (IEA, 2011). In an attempt to close this gap in a modernizing society, electricity generation is expected to increase rapidly to reach around 4,900 TWh a year by 2050 – about six times the 2010 level. Nevertheless, India's installed capacity is dominated by coal-based and gas-based thermal power (56%) followed by hydropower (23%).

Figures demonstrate that India's thermal power plants (TPPs) account for about 88% of the total industrial water demand in the country (CSE, n.d.). These mostly older generation TPPs run on open loop–wet (OLW) cooling systems with an average water use intensity around 40 to 80 times higher than the current world average for closed loop systems. Table 21.1 shows water use intensity in electricity generation under different fuel use categories and cooling types in India. While the national energy portfolio is complemented by increasing shares of natural gas and renewable energy resources, the abundance of national coal reserves means that the dominance of coal-based TPPs is not likely to change.

The environmental impact of TPPs, especially those equipped with OLW cooling systems, is a concern. These plants release above-ambient temperature cooling water into rivers and canals, causing thermal pollution and adversely affecting the aquatic ecosystems. To minimize potential damage, India's Ministry of Environment and Forests (MOEF) banned the construction of TPPs with OLW cooling systems in June 1999. The only exceptions allowed are power plants set up in coastal areas that can use seawater as a coolant. The recently introduced Zero Discharge policy also obliges operators to recirculate and reuse water in TPPs. These two regulations help to reduce the amount of water used in thermal power

TABLE 21.1 Water use intensity of thermal power plants according to fuel type and cooling system

Fuel type	Cooling type	Water use intensity of thermal power generation (m^3/MWh)
Coal	Wet cooling–open loop	80.0–160 [a]
	Wet cooling–closed loop	2.8–3.4 [b]
		(World average: 1.2–1.5 [c])
	Dry cooling	0.45–0.65 [b]
Natural gas	Wet cooling–closed loop	1.10–1.5 [b]
		3.0 [d]

Sources: [a] CSE (n.d.) and IL&FS (2009); [b] IGES (2012); [c] based on data collected from literature review and experts' interviews and compiled by the International Institute for Applied Systems Analysis (IIASA, personal communication, 1 August 2012); and [d] NEERI (2006).

generation. However, it has been estimated that around 25% of TPPs are still using OLW cooling with high water demand. Retrofitting cooling systems that conserve water in these old plants is not considered economical. Therefore, these plants will continue to function until they eventually reach the end of their designed lifespans. As Figure 21.1 shows, switching to more efficient cooling methods in TPPs would allow a reduction in water demand of about 145 billion m³ per year by 2050.

The current problem is that national planning for power generation does not fully take into account the issue of long-term water availability in the country. The findings of various basin-level studies illustrate that water availability may put the operational continuity of power plants in jeopardy. In fact, the geographical distribution of existing TPPs shows that more than 80% of these are set up in either water scarce or water stressed regions where electricity demand is expected to remain very high (Figure 21.2). Given the priority that irrigation has, followed by water for domestic use, TPPs are facing a considerable challenge to secure their required water

supply, especially during the dry season. Consequently, rainwater harvesting has become a standard proposal to win government approval for the construction of new power plants. Various scenarios (which assume medium-level economic and technological development with no stringent climate target) show that overall water demand may exceed the usable annual water availability in the country by 2050. This could further intensify existing conflicts between sectors on water use (Box 21.1). In view of the worsening situation, realigning long-term water use plans with water availability becomes a priority to avoid any potential crisis.

Clearly, the relative severity of water scarcity will vary depending on the availability of renewable freshwater resources at the local level, the trends in demographics and land use, and the political influence of water user groups. However, the fact remains that the rapid depletion of limited water resources calls for more investment in research and development. Such investment is needed notably to promote water-efficient technologies in all sectors, to carry out periodic

21.1 FIGURE **Projected water demand for electricity generation**

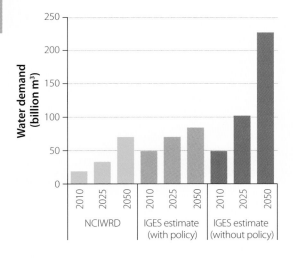

Note: The base year of the Institute for Global Environmental Strategies (IGES) model study was set at 2005 and water demand projection for electricity generation was estimated for 2010, 2025 and 2050 for comparison with National Commission on Integrated Water Resources Development (NCIWRD) projections. IGES estimates water demand for the electricity sector based only on the water use intensity of power plants. The electricity sector's water demand with policy intervention is basically considering the closed loop–wet cooling system installed after 1 June 1999 and without policy water demand is a reference estimate of continuation of use of open loop–wet cooling systems in the thermal power stations.

21.2 FIGURE **The water stress level of major river basins and the distribution of thermal power plants**

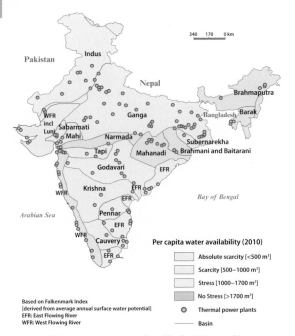

Sources: Water scarcity map developed by the Water and Resources Institute using Central Water Commission (2010) and IDFC (2011) data; and power plant location plotting done by the Institute for Global Environmental Strategies (IGES) using the Global Energy Observatory database.

water-use auditing that allows the prioritization of water conservation strategies in TPPs, and to foster better cost recovery for water services. Some positive developments indicate that there is a growing awareness of how to use limited water resources better and how to protect the environment. For example, National Water Mission (one of the key elements of the National Action Plan on Climate Change) aims to achieve a 20% increase in efficiency in water use in all sectors by 2017, and the National Green Tribunal asked MOEF to revise its area selection criteria for setting up TPPs in environmentally sensitive areas.

Conclusion

With rapid population growth, the per capita water availability in India has dipped below the alarming threshold of water stress (1,700 m³). The situation will worsen in coming years with increasing demands from the agricultural, domestic and industrial sectors. Projections made in the light of current trends show that by 2050, water demand will surpass water availability. Agriculture is, by far, the largest water user in the country and any reduction in agricultural consumption will translate into a substantial increase in water availability for other sectors and the environment. However, the energy sector also has room for improvement in reducing its water footprint. From one perspective, TPPs form the backbone of the national power supply, generating almost 60% of India's electricity. From another, almost one-quarter of existing TPPs are equipped with open loop–wet cooling systems that use 40 to 80 times more water than the world average. A gradual transition to more water-efficient cooling systems in TPPs will reduce water demand and lessen the impact on the environment. To maintain its position among the fastest growing major economies in the world, India will have to reassess its long-term water use projections in view of general water availability, and continue to improve its water use efficiency in all sectors.

Acknowledgements
Bijon Kumer Mitra, Anindya Bhattacharya

References
Except where other sources are cited, information in this chapter is adapted from:

Mitra, B.K. and Bhattacharya, A. 2013. *A Critical Review of Long Term Water–Energy Nexus in India: Case Study*. Kanagawa, Japan, Institute for Global Environmental Strategies (IGES). (Unpublished)

****

Central Water Commission. 2010. *Water and Related Statistics.* New Delhi, Ministry of Water Resources.

CSE (Center for Science and Environment). n.d. To use or to misuse: That is the question industries need to think over. *Down to Earth Supplement.* New Delhi, CSE. http://www.cseindia.org/dte-supplement/industry20040215/misuse.htm (Accessed 12 Dec 2011)

Hindustan Times. 2006. Power cuts to take care of water scarcity: Mayor. *Hindustan Times,* 22 April. http://www.hindustantimes.com/News-Feed/NM9/Powercuts-to-take-care-of-water-scarcity-Mayor/Article1-89774.aspx

IDFC (Infrastructure Development Finance Company). 2011. Water: Policy and performance for sustainable development. *India Infrastructure Report 2011.* New Delhi, Oxford University Press. http://www.idfc.com/pdf/report/IIR-2011.pdf

IEA (International Energy Agency). 2011. *Technology Development Prospects for the Indian Power Sector.* Paris, OECD/IEA. http://www.iea.org/publications/freepublications/publication/technology_development_india.pdf

IGES (Institute for Global Environmental Strategies). 2012. Survey of Indian power plants conducted during 2012. *Water Availability for Sustainable Energy Policy: Assessing Cases in South and South East Asia.* Kanagawa, Japan, IGES.

21.1

BOX

Some reported conflicts in India on the water–energy trade-off

In Madhay Pradesh, power cuts were imposed to alleviate the water shortage in the region in 2006 (*Hindustan Times,* 2006).

In Kerala, power cuts were imposed to deal with water scarcity in 2008 when monsoon rainfall was 65% less than normal (*Thaindian News,* 2008).

In Orissa, farmers protested against the increasing rate of water allocation for thermal power generation and industrial use. In response to the protest, the state government decided to give conditional permission to construct a thermal power plant that had applied to use seawater for cooling purposes rather than river water to avoid placing further pressure on the Mahanadi River basin (UNEP Finance Initiative, 2010).

Opposition to Adani power projects is growing in Nagpur. The local community believes that this power plant poses a threat to the Pench Tiger Reserves and endangers drinking water and irrigation water availability (*The Times of India,* 2011).

All six units of the Parli thermal power plant in the Beed district of Maharashtra were shut down because of a severe water shortage in the Marathwada region. The plant had previously received water from the Khadka dam, but the supply was stopped because the water level in the dam had almost dried up (NDTV, 2013).

IL&FS (Infrastructure Leasing & Financial Services Ltd). 2009. *Technical EIA Guidance Manual for Thermal Power Plants.* Prepared for the Ministry of Environment and Forests, Government of India. Hyderabad, India, IL&FS Ecosmart. http://environmentclearance.nic.in/writereaddata/Form-1A/HomeLinks/TGM_Thermal%20Power%20Plants_010910_NK.pdf

NCIWRD (National Commission on Integrated Water Resource Development). 1999. *Report of the National Commission for Integrated Water Resources Development.* New Delhi, Ministry of Water Resources.

NDTV (New Delhi Television). 2013. Maharashtra: Parli power plant shuts down after severe water crisis. NDTV website, 17 February. http://www.ndtv.com/article/india/maharashtra-parli-power-plant-shuts-down-after-severe-water-crisis-331952

NEERI (National Environmental Engineering Research Institute). 2006. *Summary Report of the Study on Post-clearance Environmental Impacts and Cost-Benefit Analysis of Power Generation in India.* Nehru Marg, India, NEERI. http://mospi.nic.in/research_studies_post_clearance.htm

Thaindian News. 2008. Kerala set to face water storage due to poor monsoon. *Thaindian News,* 7 July. http://www.thaindian.com/newsportal/business/kerala-set-toface-water-shortage-due-to-poor-monsoon_10068608.html

The Times of India. 2011. Opposition to Adani power plant in Chhindwara grows. *The Times of India,* 17 July. http://articles.timesofindia.indiatimes.com/2011-07-17/nagpur/29784634_1_adani-group-adani-power-power-plant

UNEP (United Nations Environment Programme) Finance Initiative. 2010. *Power Sector.* Chief Liquidity Series, Issue 2. Nairobi, UNEP. http://www.unepfi.org/fileadmin/documents/chief_liquidity2_01.pdf

A science-based tool for integrating geothermal resources into regional energy planning in Umbria, Italy

In many regions of the world and under a variety of geological settings, high and low temperature geothermal resources can provide concrete answers to the need for sustainable energy. Without science-based assessments however, decision-makers lack an understanding of the geothermal resources of their territories, and so are unable to take them into consideration as part of energy planning. This case study reports on the development of a science-based assessment – or 'reconnaissance'– of the geothermal potential of the Umbria region in central Italy. It can be used as an example for governments, regional and local administrations, and stakeholders from the private sector who want to integrate geothermal energy into their energy budgets. The science-based methodology that tested successfully in Umbria can help decision-makers and the private sector to (a) respond to increasing demands for energy; (b) improve sustainable economic development through the use of this renewable and environmentally safe energy source; and (c) become more involved in developing green economy approaches and technologies for power production and for other uses.

Technologies currently on the market provide commercially viable solutions for the exploitation of a wide range of geothermal waters. They cater for resources across the spectrum from low and very low enthalpy geothermal resources – which are practically ubiquitous in the earth's subsurface and can be used with geothermal heat pumps to both heat and cool – to the highly competitive and environmentally safe use of the more localized medium and high enthalpy geothermal resources for agro-industrial purposes and for power production. For example, modern, binary cycle geothermal power plants, with nearly zero emissions (Box 22.1), are able to produce electricity and heat starting from fluids at temperatures as low as about 100°C, while the conventional 'flash' geothermal power plants need fluids with temperatures of 180–200°C or above.

The assessment of the science-based methodology in Umbria followed an integrated research approach that included geological, geochemical, geophysical, three-dimensional geological and thermo-fluid-dynamic

modelling. It was largely based on existing accessible data collected since the early 1960s. It resulted in a preliminary, reconnaissance-level conceptual model of the geothermal systems located in Umbria, which will facilitate the development of projects by a wide range of potential users. The Umbria Regional Administration is using the results of this assessment to integrate geothermal energy potential into the regional sustainable energy plan, to promote its implementation by providing information and incentives, and to act as guarantor for environmental protection in the use of geothermal energy.

From the outset, the assessment was conducted with the systematic involvement of stakeholders, including local communities as well as local administrators and representatives of the private sector. A public workshop was held in March 2012 to present the objectives and the methodologies. The goal was to get feedback from local communities and stakeholders on the issues of demand and the need for thermal energy, and to listen to suggestions and proposals.

Under Italian law, geothermal resources and hydrocarbons are owned by the state and can be exploited only according to specific regulations and subject to specific

Potential for achieving significant reductions in greenhouse gas emissions

Numerical modelling simulations carried out in the five most promising areas in Umbria show that there is rich geothermal potential for electricity production as well as for providing direct heating in local districts, in agriculture (where it can be used in greenhouses, for example) and in industry. This important geothermal energy potential would deliver equally important benefits from an environmental perspective. Producing electricity with binary cycle power plants would provide annual savings equivalent to a reduction of 700,000 tonnes of carbon dioxide emissions. And using geothermal heat to its full potential to provide direct heating for the domestic, agricultural and industrial sectors would provide savings equivalent to a reduction of more than four million tonnes of carbon dioxide emissions per year. So by exploiting its geothermal resources, the Umbria Region of Italy could achieve a significant reduction in greenhouse gas emissions as well as gaining substantial economic benefits.

safeguards. To address this, the assessment also set out strategies for the sustainable management of the resource, including the fluid reinjection programmes. Italian law also takes into account the visual impact on the landscape and natural hazards that might be triggered by exploiting geothermal resources. To this end, they prescribe mandatory environmental and seismic life-cycle monitoring. So before any authorization is given to exploit these resources, an environmental impact evaluation is carried out. Both local authorities and representatives from local communities must be involved in this environmental impact assessment, and this was indeed the case in Umbria.

The assessment had already catalysed some developments on the ground. In fact, activities had been initiated for the use of geothermal fluids for power production at temperatures over 100°C. This substantially increased the percentage of power being produced from renewable sources in the Umbria region – including the direct use of the produced heat in a 'cascade' of decreasing temperature requirements.

Conclusion

The geothermal energy potential assessment realized in Umbria aims to integrate geothermal energy into the local energy budget and serve as a tool to support informed decision-making on the cost-effective use and management of the natural heat stored in aquifers. It shows how it can be harnessed for different uses, from the direct use of low temperature resources for domestic and agro-industrial purposes, to the transformation into electricity of middle to high temperature resources. The science-based methodology applied and successfully tested in Umbria will facilitate responses to society's increasing energy needs in a sustainable and environmentally friendly way.

Acknowledgements

The Regional Administration of Umbria, University of Perugia, University of Pisa

References

Information in this chapter is adapted from:

Regional Administration of Umbria, University of Perugia and University of Pisa. 2013. *Reconnaissance of the Geothermal Resources of Umbria: A Science-based Tool for the Integration of Geothermal Resources into Regional Energy Planning.* (Unpublished)

The role of hydroelectric power stations in the aftermath of the Great East Japan Earthquake

The Great East Japan Earthquake of March 2011 caused unprecedented damage to a large part of eastern Japan, particularly to the regions of Tohoku and Kanto. The majority of the damage was caused by a giant tsunami that was triggered by the earthquake. Almost 18,000 people died and 400,000 buildings suffered damage. The Fukushima Daiichi Nuclear Power Plant was severely flooded, causing it to malfunction and shut down. For similar reasons, ten other reactors also went offline almost consecutively. Furthermore, the reactors, which were already shut down at the time of disaster due to their periodic inspection, remained non-operational as a result of political pressure in the aftermath of the nuclear accident in Fukushima Daiichi. As a result, nuclear power generation dropped by almost 65% compared with same period in 2010 (Figure 23.1). The earthquake and the tsunami also affected the energy output of thermal power plants in the affected regions. Consequently, ten days of rolling blackouts started three days after the natural disaster. Radioactive contamination made recovery efforts that were already hampered by widespread blackouts even more complex.

In view of the sharp decline in the supply of power, the government requested the public in affected areas to reduce their electricity consumption by 15%. Also in line with the Electricity Business Act, a limit was put on the amount of power being consumed by commercial entities. To alleviate the energy crisis, dams in the service area of the Fukushima Daiichi nuclear power plant and those in the vicinity of Tohoku (the main disaster region) were instructed to give priority to producing the maximum amount of hydroelectricity possible.

A number of dams in the Kitakami River basin followed this directive and prioritized power generation. The Shijushida Dam operated for 24 hours on 17 March and 18 March, generating 349 MWh – or about twice its pre-earthquake output. The Gosho Dam increased its power output to 216 MWh – about 1.7 times its pre-earthquake output. The Naruko Dam, which usually stores water in mid-March (which was when the earthquake hit) for the irrigation of paddy fields, also prioritized the generation of hydroelectric power. In total, 16 dams, all directly managed by the Tohoku Regional Development Bureau at the Ministry of Land, Infrastructure, Transport and Tourism (MLIT) shifted their main use from irrigation to electricity generation to help overcome the power shortage in the afflicted areas.

To maintain a stable power supply, the Kanto Regional Development Bureau also initiated flexible dam operations on 17 March 2011 in all dams on the Sagami River basin. And by diverting flow to the Tsukui Channel, they managed to generate about 230,000 kWh of hydroelectric power – enough to meet the energy requirements of 510 households. This plan remained in operation for 45 days, until 30 April 2011.

Dams on the upper Tone River, which were originally designed to supply water to downstream areas and to maintain the river environment, were also switched to maximizing their power output. The Fujiwara hydroelectric power plant, for example, generated sufficient power for about 9,000 households. All these emergency dam operations involved careful planning that factored in reservoir replenishment by snowmelt. Weather forecasts were also monitored closely to ensure that as much power as possible could be generated and that the electricity output could be sustained.

23.1

FIGURE

Change in domestic energy supplied by nuclear power plants between 1990 and 2011

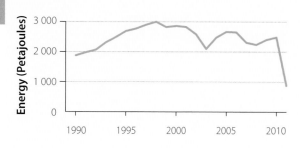

Conclusion

The Great East Japan Earthquake and the subsequent tsunami caused an unprecedented disaster. Almost 18,000 people died or are permanently unaccounted for and 400,000 buildings were damaged. In addition to the challenge of supplying drinking water to evacuees in emergency shelters, power shortages were extremely serious, and affected the entire nation. The Fukushima Daiichi Nuclear Power Plant, the main supplier of Tokyo's power, went offline after the earthquake and tsunami, and other nuclear plants were shut down soon afterwards for safety reasons. To reduce the impact of the power shortage, a series of government-led emergency measures was implemented immediately after the disaster, calling for the utmost effort on both the supply and the demand sides. The emergency dam operations in the Tohoku and Kanto regions demonstrated the versatile nature of dams that allowed a switch of priority from irrigation to power generation to alleviate electricity shortage in overwhelming circumstances.

Acknowledgements

Toshio Okazumi, Tatsuto Nakane, Takeshi Kamadai, Takashi Fukuwatari, Kazuaki Yoshida

References

Information in this chapter is adapted from:

Okazumi, T. 2013. *Water Action to Solve Energy Shortage during Great East Japan Earthquake in 2011.* Ibaraki, Japan, International Centre for Water Hazard and Risk Management (ICHARM), Public Works Research Institute. (Unpublished)

CHAPTER 24

Green energy production from municipal sewage sludge in Japan

A 15 m high tsunami, triggered by the magnitude nine Great East Japan Earthquake on 11 March 2011, caused a nuclear accident by damaging the cooling systems of three reactors in the Fukushima Daiichi Nuclear Power Plant. This event required more than 100,000 people to be evacuated from their homes (WNA, 2013). In the wake of this major incident, the promotion of green energy became one of Japan's national goals. In this process, municipal sewage sludge was identified as an untapped resource with great potential. The Japanese government was prompted to implement policies to support the development of suitable technologies to benefit from the sludge to the greatest possible extent. This case study features three leading projects where green energy is produced from municipal sewage sludge: gasification in the Tokyo Metropolitan Area, biochar production in Hiroshima City and the use of biogas as vehicle fuel and city gas in Kobe City.

24.1 Gasification in Tokyo

In 2006, the Tokyo Metropolitan Government implemented a programme to reduce greenhouse gas emissions in the area by 25% by 2020 (the year 2000 was taken as the baseline). Wastewater service activities, generating 40% of the emissions, were identified as the main challenge. The gasification of sewage sludge was proposed as an effective solution. This process converts the organic materials in wastewater into a gas mixture, which is then used as fuel for drying sludge and generating power. The high temperature in the heat recovery furnace helps to minimize the emission of nitrous oxide, which is an even more potent greenhouse agent than carbon dioxide. With the exception of a period following the Great East Japan Earthquake, the project has remained operational and met the targets set for the generation of power. However, the energy output of the dewatered sludge has been less than expected, which means that natural gas has had to be added to the fuel mix to achieve stable power generation. This aspect will require further enhancement to reduce the cost of the operation as well as to improve its environmental benefits.

24.2 Biochar production in Hiroshima

Hiroshima City had started considering biochar production as early as 2007, some four years before the 2011 earthquake. The amount of sewage sludge being generated at that time was 58,000 tonnes per year. Of this sludge, 31,000 tonnes was recycled as either compost or cement. The remainder was incinerated and used for land reclamation. However, it was subsequently considered that reclamation was not an environmentally conscious practice, and site capacity was limited. In addition, the incinerators had reached the end of their designed life and it would have been too costly to renew them. Most importantly, the unsecure disposal of sewage sludge remained a risk in view of the fluctuating need for compost and cement. Under these circumstances, Hiroshima City contracted private companies in a joint venture on a design–build–operate basis. The design and construction of the facility lasted three years and ended in March 2012. The operational period will run for 20 years – up to 2032.

The contractor handles 28,000 tonnes of dewatered sludge per year in a plant that has a daily capacity of 100 tonnes. The project uses low-temperature (250°C to 350°C) carbonization technology, which allows the production of biochar that has a high calorie, low risk of self-ignition and a low odour level. In the first six months of operation (April to September 2012), 14,000 tonnes of dewatered sludge was processed and 2,300 tonnes of biochar was produced. From an environmental perspective, the use of biogas (which is generated as part of the sludge dewatering process) as a fuel to produce biochar reduced the annual greenhouse gas emissions (carbon dioxide) of the city's wastewater services by 12%. Furthermore, using biochar at coal-fired power plants is expected to reduce yearly greenhouse gas emission by another 9%.

24.3 Biogas as vehicle fuel and city gas in Kobe

Six wastewater treatment plants in Kobe treat approximately 500,000 m³ sewage per day, generating 37,000 m³ biogas. Because of its poor quality, this combustible gas was mainly used on site to heat digester tanks. But in an attempt to reduce greenhouse gas emissions in the city, the Kobe City authorities started to supply biogas as an auto fuel and also mixed it into the city's gas supply in purified form.

One example of how this works is the wastewater treatment plant at Higashinada, which generates 10,000 Nm^3 (normal cubic metres)[1] biogas per day. Following the purification process, 20% of the biogas is used to fuel vehicles, 45% is used in the in the wastewater treatment plant in which it is generated, and the remainder goes through a second level of purification before being fed into the city gas supply. Overall, the project produces 800,000 Nm^3 biogas per year, which is equivalent to the annual gas consumed by 2,000 households. The project has resulted in a reduction of 1,200 tonnes of carbon dioxide emissions per year.

Conclusion

The nuclear disaster at Fukushima Daiichi in 2011 brought renewed attention to ways of producing green energy. Three case studies – from the Tokyo Metropolitan Area, Hiroshima City and Kobe City – show innovative ways of generating energy by using biogas and biochar derived from municipal sewage. The methods being used have also helped to reduce environmental pollution by reducing greenhouse gas emissions and decreasing the amount of waste that these municipalities need to dispose of into nature. Technological improvement is likely to further increase efficiency in the methods described and pave the way for a wider adoption of programmes that turn common waste into a rich green energy resource.

Acknowledgements

Yosuke Matsumiya, Kazuaki Yoshida

References

Except where other sources are cited, information in this chapter is adapted from:

Matsumiya, Y. 2013. *Green Energy Production from Municipal Sewage Sludge in Japan.* Prepared by the International Division, Technical Department, Japan Sewage Works Association. Tokyo, Global Center for Urban Sanitation (GCUS). http://tinyurl.com/oe5frsv (Accessed Jul 2013)

****

WNA (World Nuclear Association). n.d. *Fukushima Accident.* London, WNA. http://www.world-nuclear.org/info/Safety-and-Security/Safety-of-Plants/Fukushima-Accident (Accessed Oct 2013)

---

1   Normal cubic metres (Nm^3) describes the volume of gas under standard temperature and pressure conditions.

CHAPTER

25

The role of geothermal energy in Kenya's long-term development vision

In Kenya, the rate of electrification is around 16%, among the lowest rates in sub-Saharan Africa. The state-owned Kenya Electricity Generating Company Limited (KenGen) is the major energy utility and produces 80% of the electricity used in the country. Its 14 hydroelectric power stations account for almost half of the national electricity supply. Heavy reliance on hydropower has, however, made Kenya's power supply susceptible to variations in rainfall. With droughts becoming more frequent, water and power shortages are affecting all sectors of the economy. For example, the drought that occurred between 1999 and 2002 had a drastic impact on the hydropower plants and caused a 25% reduction in the amount of electricity generated in 2000 (Karekezi et al., 2009). The resultant cumulative economic loss was estimated to be about 1% to 1.5% of the total Gross Domestic Product, roughly US$442 million (Karekezi and Kithyoma, 2005).

As a stop-gap measure, the government engages private energy companies that generate electricity using imported fossil fuels such as coal and diesel. This option has proved to be costly because of the rising prices of such fuels in international markets. It also leads to considerable air pollution from diesel generators (GDC, 2013).

While only one in five Kenyans has access to electricity (IEA, 2011), rapidly rising demand is expected to outstrip supply over the coming years. To address this challenge – while still keeping a low carbon footprint – the energy sector has focused on renewable resources in line with Vision 2030, which is the blueprint for the country's transformation into a middle income nation by 2030 (Box 25.1).

The successful implementation of the Vision greatly depends on the supply of adequate, reliable, clean and affordable energy. The energy sector is expected to remain a key player in the overall improvement of the general welfare of the population, which includes the international goal of halving poverty by 2015. The Ministry of Energy will facilitate this by creating an enabling environment for private sector-led growth in energy supply. The key steps in achieving this target are identified as licensing firms to explore geothermal fields, formulating policy and developing an appropriate legal and regulatory framework.

The exploitation of geothermal resources is one of the critical elements of Kenya's Vision 2030 growth strategy. Its main advantages over other sources of energy are that it is indigenous, output is not affected by climatic variability and it has no adverse effects on the environment. Geothermal fields located within the country's Rift Valley have the potential to produce an estimated 14,000 MW. This rich source has not been adequately tapped: the installed geothermal capacity corresponds to just 1.5% of the country's potential (ERC, n.d.). Ongoing projects are geared towards meeting the Vision 2030 medium-term target of 1,600 MW by 2016, and eventually 5,000 MW of geothermal power by 2030 (Table 25.1). This would account for one-quarter of Kenya's total installed capacity, and would be a substantial increase on the 2012 figure of 10%.

To attract investment in energy production, the government introduced the Energy Act in 2006. The Act established the Energy Regulatory Commission (ERC), set up to enforce and review environmental quality standards in coordination with other statutory agencies. The Geothermal Development Company (GDC) was formed in 2009 under the same Act and under the National Energy Policy Sessional Paper 4 of 2004. The GDC is a government body that aims to promote the rapid development of geothermal resources in Kenya to meet the 2030 geothermal energy target. In this critical function, the GDC aims to cushion investors from the high capital investment risks associated with drilling geothermal wells. The GDC is expected to drill as many as 1,400 wells to explore steam prospects and make productive wells available to successful bidding investors from both public and private power companies. It is envisaged that the successful bidders will use them to generate electricity or for other uses, such as in greenhouses that use heat and carbon dioxide for photosynthesis and hydrogen sulphide fumigation to improve plant productivity. The Menengai Crater lies at the centre of the GDC's most recent exploration activities. This geothermal field is estimated to have the potential to produce 1,600 MW (*Daily Nation*, 2010), practically equivalent to the current national power supply (GDC, 2011).

Ongoing public and private investments are planned to increase geothermal power production by 500 MW by the end of 2014. It is estimated that reaching the goal of 5,000 MW geothermal power by 2030 will require an investment of US$20 billion (Ecomagination, 2011). In the fiscal year budget for 2012–2013, geothermal and coal exploration and development activities were allocated US$340 million (Kivuva, 2012). Of this amount, the GDC was allocated only US$20 million (Republic of Kenya, 2012).

Conclusion

Kenya set an ambitious Vision in 2008 that aims to raise the country out of poverty and turn it into a middle income nation by 2030. In Vision 2030, energy plays a key role as one of the infrastructural enablers upon which the economic, social and political pillars of the country's development will be built. While energy is very important for Kenya's development, the country's reliance on hydropower as the major supply for electricity has caused frequent blackouts and power rationing linked to droughts and variations in water availability in dam reservoirs. This has left the government without any choice but to use expensive emergency generators that run on imported fuels. The Kenyan government has opted for the development of geothermal energy as a key response to overcome the country's energy bottleneck. This option is not only environmentally friendly, but also provides additional benefits such as reducing the cost of imported fuel, and stimulating the economy through investing in clean energy. In line with the Vision 2030 document, the Ministry of Energy set a specific target that by 2030, geothermal power would account for one-quarter of Kenya's total installed capacity – up from the current level of 10%. This target will require considerable investment that calls for private sector involvement. To tackle this challenge, the GDC was created in 2009 to cover the high cost of steam well exploration, thereby reducing the risk for potential investors. Achieving its plans for geothermal energy is critical if Kenya is to elevate its economy into middle income status and set an example for the rest of the region.

TABLE 25.1

Vision 2030 energy generation projection by source

Energy source	Capacity (MW)	Percentage of total
Geothermal	5 530	26
Nuclear	4 000	18
Coal	2 720	13
Gas turbines/natural gas	2 340	11
Diesel turbines	1 955	9
Import	2 000	9
Wind	2 036	9
Hydropower	1 039	5
Total	**21 620**	**100**

Source: Kianji (2012).

Acknowledgements

Ezekiel Kemboi, Chrispine Omondi Juma

References

Except where other sources are cited, information in this chapter is adapted from:

Kemboi, E. (Kenya Electricity Generating Company Limited) and Juma, C.O. (Ministry of Water and Irrigation, Kenya). 2013. *Water Resources and Geothermal Energy Development in Kenya.* (Unpublished)

****

Daily Nation. 2010. All set for Kenya geothermal project. *Daily Nation,* 24 October. http://www.nation.co.ke/business/news/All%20set%20for%20Kenya%20geothermal%20project/-/1006/1039550/-/jriv2y/-/

Ecomagination. 2011. *Full Steam Ahead: Kenya's Geothermal Production Picks Up Speed.* Fairfield, CT, General Electric. http://www.ecomagination.com/full-steam-ahead-kenyas-geothermal-production-picks-up-speed

ERC (Energy Regulatory Commission). n.d. *Geothermal Energy, Renewables* home page. Nairobi, ERC. http://www.erc.go.ke/index.php?option=com_fsf&view=faq&catid=2&Itemid=649 (Accessed Sep 2013)

GDC (Geothermal Development Company). 2011. *Kenya Geothermal Company Finds Exploitable Steam in Menengai.* Nairobi, GDC. http://tinyurl.com/o982ebk

————. n.d. Home page. Nairobi, GDC. http://www.gdc.co.ke/index.php?option=com_content&view=article&id=139&Itemid=203 (Accessed Sep 2013)

IEA (International Energy Agency). 2011. *World Energy Outlook* Electricity Access Database. Paris, OECD/IEA. http://www.iea.org/media/weowebsite/energydevelopment/WEO-2011_new_Electricity_access_Database.xls

Karekezi, S., Kimani, J., Onguru, O. and Kithyoma, W. 2009. *Large Scale Hydropower, Renewable Energy Adaptation and Climate Change: Climate Change and Energy Security in East and Horn of Africa.* Occasional Paper No. 33. Nairobi, Energy, Environment and Development Network for Africa (AFREPREN/FWD). http://www.ke.boell.org/downloads/RenewableEnergyandAdaptationtoClimateChangePublication.pdf

Karekezi, S. and Kithyoma, W. (eds). 2005. *Sustainable Energy in Africa: Cogeneration and Geothermal in the East and Horn of Africa: Status and Prospects.* Nairobi, AFREPREN/FWD.

Ketraco (Kenya Electricity Transmission Co. Ltd). n.d. Vision 2030. Nairobi, Ketraco. http://www.ketraco.co.ke/about/vision2030.html (Accessed Sep 2013)

Kianji, C.K. 2012. *Kenya's Energy Demand and the Role of Nuclear Energy in Future Energy Generation Mix.* Paper presented at the Joint JAPAN–IAEA Nuclear Energy Management School in Tokai-mura, Japan, 11–29 June 2012. http://www.iaea.org/nuclearenergy/nuclearknowledge/schools/NEM-school/2012/Japan/PDFs/week2/CR6_Kenya.pdf

Kivuva, E. 2012. *Is Infrastructure Budget the Solution to Economic Growth?* Nairobi, Kenya Engineer. http://www.kenyaengineer.co.ke/index.php/mr/77-top-projctes/559-is-infrastructure-budget-the-solution-for-economic-growth

Republic of Kenya. 2012. *Medium-Term Budget Policy Statement.* Nairobi, Ministry of Finance.

26 The Four Major Rivers Restoration Project as a part of the National Green Growth Strategy in Republic of Korea

Since the 1960s, the Republic of Korea has enjoyed rapid development. Throughout this period, water use has increased sixfold and the intensive industrialization efforts have made Korea the world's fourth largest energy importer (IEA, 2012). In view of the swiftly growing demands for both resources, the government has taken concrete steps to develop policies to adopt an integrated approach to managing water and energy. Among those policies is the Green New Deal, introduced in 2009 with a US$38 billion investment portfolio over four years. In broad terms, it focuses on four main themes: environmental protection, energy conservation, information technology infrastructure for the future and green neighbourhoods and housing (UNESCAP, 2012). This case study on the Four Major Rivers Restoration Project (4MRRP) features one of the projects conducted under the first theme, and puts the emphasis particularly on the small hydropower plants that were put into operation in 16 weirs.

The country's green growth strategy, which started in 2008, sets out a new vision to reduce energy dependency by diversifying energy sources. As a part of this approach, the First National Energy Master Plan (2008–2030) introduced an Act encouraging the promotion of new and renewable sources of energy. The aim was to increase the proportion of energy derived from renewable resources fivefold – from 2.2% in 2006 to 11% by 2030 (Table 26.1). Among the renewable energy sources that are being considered are hydropower, solar power, geothermal power and energy from organic sources.

Similar to energy, water resources development has always been a national priority. This necessity stems from the challenge that seasonal distribution of rainfall shows a large discrepancy (more than 70% of annual average precipitation falls in four months during the flood season between June and September) thus limiting the availability of this precious resource throughout the year (MLTM, 2011). Consequently, from the mid-1960s up to the 1980s, government policies centred on developing large infrastructure, including construction of numerous multipurpose dams to supply water and generate hydroelectricity. Now, facing the challenges caused by climate change and in a bid to reduce the country's dependence on imported energy, additional dams and hydraulic structures are being built while existing ones are being revisited to improve their efficiency and to bring further functionality.

TABLE 26.1 Primary energy demand and supply targets for 2030 by source

Demand	Oil (%)	Coal (%)	Liquefied natural gas (%)	Nuclear (%)	Other (%)
2006	43.6	24.3	13.7	15.9	2.5
2030[BAU]	34.2	24.7	15.8	19.5	5.9
2030[target]	33.0	15.7	12.0	27.8	11.5

Supply	New and renewables excluding hydropower (%)
2006	2.2
2030[target]	11

Note: BAU, business as usual. 'Other' consists of hydropower and new and renewable sources.
Source: Third National Energy Committee (2008).

The 4MRRP (Box 26.1) is a recent example of such efforts. As part of this multipurpose green growth project, 16 weirs each with a small hydropower plant were built on the Han, Nakdong, Geum and Yeongsan rivers. The total installed capacity of 50 MWh provided by the 16 hydropower plants' 41 generators is equivalent to one-quarter that of the largest hydropower plant in Korea. Annual electricity generation is sufficient to meet the energy requirements of more than 58,000 households. The capacity replaces use of over 60,000 tonnes (450,000 barrels) of oil per year – or an emission reduction of some 180,000 tonnes of carbon dioxide. Aside from its environmental and economic benefits, the project also allows for the development of domestic green technologies. In January 2013, the small hydropower plants on the four rivers were registered as Clean Development Mechanism projects with the United Nations Framework Convention on Climate Change (UNFCCC).

Conclusion

Water-related disasters have become more frequent and severe in Korea as a result of global climate change. These disasters have caused fluctuations in freshwater availability and have also brought about financial losses for the country. The other side of the coin is that as the fourth largest energy importer in the world, Korea itself is contributing to climate change through greenhouse gas

---

26.1
BOX

The Four Major Rivers Restoration Project

The Four Major Rivers Restoration Project (4MRRP), which is the showcase element of Korea's Green New Deal plan, involved both improving existing waterworks and building complementary ones (see highlights below). The project was completed for the most part in December 2012. One of its main functions, flood protection, had been put to the test when Typhoon Meari caused extensive damage to the west of the country in June 2011. In spite of the heavy downpour – which brought over 200 mm of rain (about 16% of the annual average) to much of the country over six days – there was no significant flood damage.

The project also created jobs. According to the Ministry of Labour, 90,000 new positions were put in place thanks to the 4MRRP. Its economic benefits are expected to grow as investment into research and development for the project as well as into its operation and management continues.

Highlights of the 4MRRP

Project period:
October 2009–December 2012

Project area:
Han, Nakdong, Geum and Yeongsan rivers
(see the map to the right)

Core tasks:
• Securing freshwater availability
• Flood protection
• Water quality improvement and restoration of river ecosystems
• Development of recreational areas and multi-purpose spaces
• Community development centred on rivers

Major works:
• 450 million m³ sediment removed by dredging
• 16 weirs constructed
• 784 km of river banks reinforced
• Two new dams built
• Two flood retention reservoirs constructed

Budget:
US$19 billion

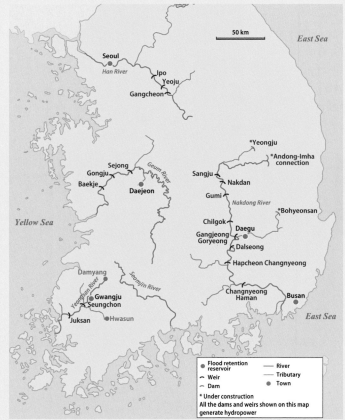

emissions. As a result, since 2008, the government has been formulating policies for green growth to reduce its carbon footprint, prepare the country to deal with the effects of climate change, and maintain its good water management practices. The Green New Deal, initiated in 2009, comes with an economic package for investment in green growth. A part of the Green New Deal, the 4MRRP aims to revitalize the Han, Nakdong, Geum and Yeongsan rivers to improve water availability and quality, control floods, restore ecosystems and promote nature-conscious development. The 16 weirs and 41 hydropower-generating units that were built during the project constitute an important part of the 4MRRP. They are designed to store optimal amounts of water for generating energy, without interrupting the natural flow of the rivers. While the amount of electricity generated is modest, the project represents Korea's firm commitment to reduce greenhouse gas emissions as a part of its low carbon green growth policies.

Acknowledgements

Kyung-Jin Min, Tae-sun Shin, Ji-eun Seong

References

Except where other sources are cited, information in this chapter is adapted from:

Min, K-J., Shin, T-s. and Seong, J-e. 2013. *Small Hydro Power Plants of the 4 Major Rivers: Korea's Green Growth Initiatives in the Water-Energy Sector.* Daejeon, Korea, Korea Water Resources Corporation (K-Water) Research Institute. (Unpublished)

****

IEA (International Energy Agency). 2012. Selected indicators for 2010. *Key World Energy Statistics 2012,* pp. 48–57. Paris, OECD/IEA.

MLTM (Ministry of Land Transport and Marine Affairs, Korea). 2011. [The Ministry of Land, Transport, and Maritime Affairs releases directions for water policy by field until 2020.] Press release, 28 December. (In Korean)

Third National Energy Committee. 2008. *First National Energy Master Plan: 2008–2030.* Seoul, Government of the Republic of Korea. (In Korean)

UNESCAP (United Nations Economic and Social Commission for Asia and the Pacific). 2012. *Low Carbon Green Growth Roadmap for Asia and the Pacific. Fact Sheet: Green New Deal.* Bangkok, UNESCAP. http://www.unescap.org/esd/environment/lcgg/documents/roadmap/case_study_fact_sheets/Fact%20Sheets/FS-Green-New-Deal%20.pdf

CHAPTER 27

Solar powered wastewater treatment plant in Mexico

The city of Nogales in Sonora, Mexico, shares the international border to the north with the United States city of Nogales in Santa Cruz County, Arizona. From 1951, both municipalities relied on a wastewater treatment plant in neighbouring Rio Rico, Arizona, adjacent to the confluence of the Santa Cruz River and the Nogales Wash. Both countries funded the plant proportionally, on the basis of their respective flow contributions to the facility (IBWC, n.d.).

Approximately 80% of the wastewater treated at the facility came from the much larger Mexican Nogales. Cost considerations led the city in 2010 to initiate construction of the Los Alisos Wastewater Treatment Plant (WWTP) on Mexican territory – a US$20 million project that now benefits 70,000 inhabitants. The plant's effluent is discharged into the Los Alisos stream, which flows to the south where it is utilized for irrigation and aquifer recharge.

Environmental sustainability is an important, cross-cutting public policy issue in Mexico, and solar energy has long been a recognized alternative energy option throughout the country, albeit seldom utilized. To date, solar technologies have most commonly been used in rural communities that lack access to centralized water supply and electricity services. To promote further developments in this area, however, Mexico's Environment and Natural Resources Sector Program established guidelines on renewable energy sources. This was followed in 2008 by Mexico's Law on the Use of Renewable Energies and Energy Transition Funding, which encouraged mainstream public policies to promote the development and use of renewable energy sources.

Drawing on the National Water Commission's (CONAGUA) experience with renewable energies, a solar panel farm was incorporated into the Los Alisos WWTP project, offering financial and environmental benefits. Design of the photovoltaic segment began in May 2011 with a detailed study of various configuration alternatives. The selected project covers an area of 15,000 m², in which 3,920 solar panels will generate 1,500,000 kWh/year. Although the electricity output of solar panel farm will vary throughout the year depending on solar radiation intensity (Figure 27.1), the annual average energy

27.1 **FIGURE** **Average energy budget of Los Alisos Wastewater Treatment Plant upon completion of the solar panel farm**

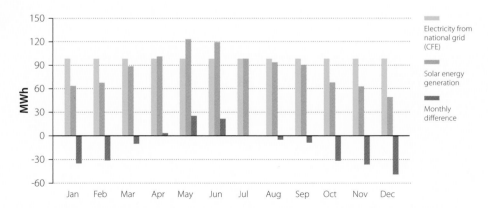

Note: Negative values denote that solar energy generation is not sufficient for the operation of the Wastewater Treatment Plant (WWTP). The difference is obtained from the national power grid. Positive values signify that the solar panels generate more energy than required by the WWTP. The excess amount is fed into the national grid.

generation will be approximately equal to that required to power the WWTP. A permanent connection to the national power grid (managed by the Federal Electricity Commission of Mexico) will serve a dual purpose: feeding energy into the plant to ensure that Los Alisos functions 24 hours a day throughout the year (including night time, cloudy periods and winter months) and feeding excess energy generated in the summer months back into the national grid.

The Los Alisos WWTP is already operational; however, construction of the solar panel farm began in November 2012 and is expected to be completed by early 2014, at an estimated cost of US$5 million. Currently, no comparable projects have been initiated in Mexico or elsewhere in Latin America.

Conclusion

The Los Alisos WWTP in Mexico demonstrates a practical implementation of the use of solar energy. Due to ongoing construction of the solar panel farm, the plant is currently running on electricity from Mexico's national power grid, but it will be practically energy self-sufficient on completion of its photovoltaic segment. Serving over 70,000 habitats by cleaning and reclaiming approximately 6.5 million m³ wastewater per year, the Los Alisos WWTP is the first of its kind in Latin America. This innovative project and the development of similar WWTPs in the future will help communities to become more sustainable.

Acknowledgement

The National Water Commission of Mexico (CONAGUA)

References

Except where other sources are cited, information in this chapter is adapted from:

CONAGUA (National Water Commission of Mexico). 2013. *Solar Power for the Wastewater Treatment Plant 'Los Alisos' in Nogales, Sonora: Case Study.* Mexico DF, CONAGUA. (Unpublished)

****

IBWC (International Boundary and Water Commission, United States and Mexico). n.d. *Nogales Field Office and Wastewater Treatment Plant.* http://www.ibwc.state.gov/Organization/ Operations/Field_Offices/Nogales.html (Accessed Oct 2013)

Water and energy linkage in Austin, Texas, USA

Austin, home of the state government, is situated near the centre of energy-rich and water-stressed Texas. It has been among the fastest growing major cities in the United States of America (USA) for much of the past decade, with an estimated population in 2011 of 820,000 – which represents growth of more than 80% since 1990 (Toohey, 2012). This rapid growth continues to put pressure on the public electricity and water suppliers, Austin Energy and Austin Water, to provide reliable services while also promoting environmental sustainability and fiscal responsibility. Communication and cooperation between these two entities, while also enabling public engagement, helps to drive innovation in the fields of energy and water conservation.

Historically, Austin has relied on the Colorado River, which runs through the state, as its sole water source. A new, reclaimed water programme is now providing around 2% of supply. The city has pre-purchased rights to divert 360 million m³ water per year from the Colorado River for municipal use. A new treatment plant is under construction and is expected to be in operation in 2014. This will add 200,000 m³ capacity to the water supply system each day. Austin Water serves 200,000 connections over an area of approximately 1,400 km².

Austin Energy is the eighth-largest public electricity utility in the USA, with a diverse generation capacity

of over 3,100 MW (Table 28.1). The utility serves more than 400,000 customers, approximately 90% of whom are residential users.

Austin Water is Austin Energy's fifth-largest consumer, using 210,000 MWh electricity to pump and treat 300 million m³ water, including 100 million m³ wastewater (Austin Energy, n.d.).

Energy and water conservation initiatives have their origins in both city policy and citizen-led efforts. For example, housed within Austin Energy, the Green Building programme has guided resource use efficiency in Austin since 1990. A citizen driven effort to stop a large development being built over a local aquifer the same year catalysed the adoption of the city's Save Our Springs ordinance in 1992 – an initiative that has shaped development patterns while also ensuring sustainable use of water resources and protecting their quality.

To optimize water and energy use while keeping costs down, both supply-side and demand-side measures are taken at the city level. For example, Austin Water and Austin Energy constantly measure critical parameters such as the amount of energy used in providing water services, water use in thermoelectricity generation and the average water use in water and energy services. Ongoing efforts in place since the 1980s conserve water and electricity. They have brought about a reduction in demand (Box 28.1) and this has allowed both Austin Energy and Austin Water to postpone building major new facilities. In fact, Austin Energy has invested in demand-side conservation of 700 MW with an additional 800 MW peak-day demand target by 2020. Over the same period, comprehensive water conservation efforts, including a tiered rate structure and weekly watering schedules for landscaped areas, have helped to reduce peak seasonal demand and keep daily residential water consumption levels below 400 litres per person on average. The city's free distribution of high-efficiency kitchen and bathroom aerators and showerheads, along with rebates to eligible groups buying high-efficiency dishwashers, washing machines, auxiliary water and irrigation system upgrades,

28.1 TABLE	**Austin Energy resources and generation capacities in 2013**	
	Type	**Capacity (MW)**
	Coal	600
	Nuclear	400
	Gas	1 544
	Biomass	12
	Wind	560
	Solar	31

has added further energy savings by reducing customers' end-use energy for heating and on-site pumping (ACEEE, n.d.).

The two utilities also collaborate in generating renewable energy and reducing greenhouse gas emissions: an innovative thin-film rooftop solar panel system has offset the energy demand of the Austin Water service centre (approximately 7,000 m^2) since late 2010. Likewise, a cogeneration system that uses biogas generated at the city's Hornsby Bend wastewater sludge treatment plant meets that facility's entire energy requirements for electricity and heat. It also has the additional real potential – which is still being investigated – to provide compressed natural gas for its own equipment and transport demands, which would result in an essentially net-zero-energy facility. To further reduce its carbon emissions, Austin Water switched in 2011 to Austin Energy's 100% wind energy programme, Green Choice. This allowed an 85% reduction in the water utility's greenhouse gas emissions. The remaining 15% is related to transport and direct emissions of methane and nitrous oxide from the treatment processes. As a part of its environmentally conscious service policy, Austin Water reduces its energy requirement during times of peak electricity demand in order to reduce grid loads.

Finally, Austin Water and Austin Energy are both participants in the Pecan Street Project, an integrated smart-grid demonstration and research effort based in Austin and run in partnership with the University of Texas at Austin and other key stakeholders in energy,

water and sustainability (Pecan Street Research Institute, 2010). In a study being conducted over a five-year period, project participants are testing how smart metering of the consumption of electricity, water and gas, in concert with interventions like smart appliances, management systems and pricing models, can change the way households use utility services – and may change the way utilities engage with each other and with their customers.

Conclusion

The Austin, Texas case study illustrates how a fast-growing major US city with publicly owned water and electricity utilities can craft integrative and strategic programmes and policies that help to meet the needs of the public while also helping each sector. Initiatives promoting the efficient use of water and electricity over the past two decades have allowed utilities to postpone major supply expansion efforts; although with the city's continued growth, both water and electricity utilities are expanding their supply capacity while carrying on with their demand reduction and management efforts. Several recent and ongoing projects highlight the cooperation between the two utilities and the opportunities for synergies across sectors. Austin Water's reclaimed water programme reduces overall surface water withdrawals and provides water at a low cost to energy generation facilities operated by Austin Energy and the University of Texas. Austin Water has tracked its energy use both spatially and temporally in order to come to a better understanding of the energy embedded in its services and to identify opportunities in emerging energy markets. Austin Energy reports on the energy savings associated

---

28.1 BOX

Water and energy conservation efforts in Austin

Since 2006, reclaimed water has been pumped to Austin Energy's Sand Hill Energy Center from the nearby South Austin Regional wastewater treatment plant. Once on site, the water is further processed to be used as coolant for the combined-cycle power generation unit. Austin Energy completed a pilot study in January 2013 to test the feasibility of using reclaimed water for other systems that currently require tap water. The results were favourable, and by 2015, the percentage of reclaimed water being used is expected to increase. In addition to consuming less water, the subsidized rate of the reclaimed water, which is approximately 10% of the cost of tap water, will save the Sand Hill Energy Center money (Jake Spelman, Austin Energy, personal communication). And because Sand Hill is located next to the South Austin Regional wastewater treatment plant, Austin Water estimates the energy needed to transport the reclaimed water is around 40% less than the energy needed to provide potable water from more distant facilities.

Another notable example of water and energy working together is at the University of Texas flagship campus in Austin, which operates its own 140 MW power plant. The campus was connected to Austin Water's reclaimed water programme in April 2013, which allowed it to use reclaimed water for irrigation on the campus, to cool its power plant and to provide air conditioning to the campus through a chilled water infrastructure.

with reduced water consumption. Both utility companies are participating in smart grid demonstration efforts such as the Pecan Street Project, which will provide residential customers with consumption information and management technologies for better and sustainable use of valuable water and energy resources.

Acknowledgements

David Greene, Jake Spelman, Jill Kjelsson

References

Except where other sources are cited, information in this chapter is adapted from:

Greene, D. (Austin Water), Spelman, J. (Austin Energy) and Kjelsson, J. (University of Texas, Austin). 2013. *Water and Energy in Austin, Texas.* (Unpublished)

****

ACEEE (American Council for an Energy-Efficient Economy). n.d. *City of Austin: Multifamily Energy and Water Efficiency Program.* Washington DC, ACEEE. http://aceee.org/w-e-program/city-austin-multifamily-energy-and-wat (Accessed Oct 2013)

Austin Energy. n.d. *Austin Energy FY2014–2018 Financial Forecast.* Austin, TX, Austin Energy. http://www.yumpu.com/en/document/view/13766054/austin-energy (Accessed Oct 2013)

Pecan Street Research Institute. 2010. *What is Pecan Street?* Austin, TX, Pecan Street Inc. http://www.pecanstreet.org/about/what-is-pecan-street-inc/

Toohey, M. 2012. *Austin Property Taxes Jump 38% Over Past Decade.* Statesman.com. http://www.statesman.com/news/news/local/austin-property-taxes-jump-38-over-past-decade/nRprf/

29

The use of and prospects for geothermal energy in Turkey

Turkey is an emerging market country, and the world's seventeenth largest economy (MFA, 2013). As part of its process of rapid growth and industrialization, Turkey's energy demand is forecast to grow by 6% to 8% annually by 2020, requiring an additional 50,000 MW to be added to the national grid (Lally, 2011).

However, the country is energy poor, and the vast majority of domestic demand is met by importing fossil fuel. This imposes a significant burden on the economy. The national energy bill in 2012 was US$60 billion, which was an 11% increase on 2011 (Hürriyet, 2013). Because this trend seems certain to continue, the diversification of Turkey's energy supply is critical. In contrast to its limited oil and gas reserves, Turkey has a range of renewable energy resources, including access to wind power, hydropower, solar power, geothermal energy and biomass. Notably, Turkey is ranked as the seventh most promising country in the world in terms of geothermal energy potential (GEA, 2012). With proper planning and sufficient investment, its rich geothermal resources can help to lessen its dependence on external sources of energy (Box 29.1). The advantage of geothermal energy is that it is clean and releases negligible amounts of greenhouse gas – if any at all – into the atmosphere. Its use in homes and in commercial operations has shown that it can account for savings as high as 80% when compared with using fossil fuels (US DOE, 2013).

Turkey's first ventures into geothermal research were initiated by the national institutions in the 1960s. While a thorough exploration and evaluation is yet to be completed, over 200 low to medium enthalpy geothermal fields have been discovered in various locations. These fields contain fluid and steam at temperatures lower than 200°C, which makes them suitable for direct use applications such as district heating, space heating, balneology, aquaculture and greenhouse heating. Of these, district heating is one of the main applications of geothermal energy in Turkey. The first of these systems was set up in 1983. Then, between 1991 and 2006, 19 additional district heating systems were installed (Serpen et al., 2010). The biggest one in İzmir-Balçova has equivalent heating capacity for 35,000 residences.

In view of the growing demand for electricity, the Turkish government introduced Law 5346 and Law 5686. Law 5346, the Renewable Energy Law, entered into force in 2005 and deals with the use of renewable energy resources for the purpose of electrical power generation. It sets a fixed feed-in tariff for various energy resources, and gives incentives for renewables. It also encourages the local governorships and municipalities to benefit from the geothermal resources within their jurisdictions by building and operating geothermal district heating systems. The Amending Law 6094 came into effect in 2011 to introduce further incentives to encourage investments.

29.1

BOX

The importance of geothermal energy in Turkey

Almost 80% of Turkey's energy consumption is met by imports. The extent of this reliance – particularly on natural gas – threatens the essentials of the country's sustainable development model seriously. Added to this, Turkey's continued dependence on fossil fuels will contribute to global warming and to rapid worsening of the environment and air quality in the country. In this context, geothermal energy has a major contribution to make to Turkey's energy diversification strategy. If it were to use its geothermal potential fully, Turkey would be capable of meeting 5% of its electricity needs and 30% of its heat requirements from geothermal sources – which corresponds to 14% of its total energy needs. Generally speaking, the cost of producing geothermal power is higher than that of classic fuels (US EIA, 2013). However, cost comparisons are highly subject to fluctuation, and the ongoing efforts for advances in geothermal power production technologies may make this cost relationship more favourable for geothermal energy (Erdoğdu, 2009).

Law 5686, known as the Geothermal Law, was passed in 2007. It deals with geothermal resources and natural mineral waters. Among the purposes of this Law are to set rules and principles for the search for and exploration, development and production of geothermal resources. It also sets rules for the protection of these resources, including regulations that govern how to make economic use of them in compliance with environment protection guidelines, and sets out how they should be reclaimed after use.

As a result of these laws, Turkey's capacity for geothermal electricity production has increased by more than 100% since 2009 (Figure 29.1). Most of this growth has been realized by the private sector. The installed capacity is expected to reach 750 MWe by the end of 2018 (Table 29.1). Concerning other uses of geothermal energy, at the end of 2012, Turkey had an installed capacity of 2,705 MWt for direct use applications – a 30% increase on 2010 values. Overall, geothermal district heating projects have been

put into use in 16 cities and are expected to grow fivefold in capacity between 2014 and 2018. While reaching the 2018 targets (Table 29.1) requires an investment of approximately US$5 billion, the economic value to be generated is estimated to be around US$32 billion per year. It is also expected to create employment for 300,000 people.

The use of geothermal energy has proved to be environmentally friendly and economically competitive when compared with fossil fuel alternatives. For example, in Turkey, geothermal heating typically costs 60% less than its natural gas equivalent. Overall, the country's current installed capacity of geothermal energy allows an annual saving of approximately US$1 billion, which would otherwise have to be spent on importing natural gas.

Conclusion

In 2012, Turkey spent US$60 billion on gas and oil imports to meet the energy demands of its swiftly growing economy. This bill will continue to rise in parallel with increasing energy use in the country and the price of fuel on the international markets. Given its considerable potential to generate energy from wind, hydropower, solar power, geothermal resources and biomass, renewable energy constitutes a plausible alternative to fossil fuels. Among these, geothermal energy deserves special attention as Turkey is ranked the seventh most promising country in the world in terms of its rich potential. As a result of the legal framework set by Law 5346, Law 5686 and Law 6094, the private sector has been actively involved in developing geothermal fields to generate electricity and for direct-use applications such as district heating, greenhouse heating and in thermal

FIGURE 29.1

Trend in geothermal electricity production

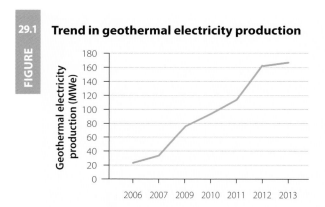

Source: Mertoğlu and Başarır (2013).

TABLE 29.1

Use of geothermal resources in Turkey, and projections for 2018

Type of utilization	Installed capacity (2012)	2018 Projections
Geothermal district heating	89 443 residences equivalence (805 MWt)	500 000 residences equivalence (4 000 MWt)
Greenhouse heating	2 832 000 m² (612 MWt)	6 000 000 m² (2 040 MWt)
Balneological use	350 thermal facilities equivalence (870 MWt) (16 million visitors annually)	400 thermal facilities equivalence (1 100 MWt)
Electricity generation	168 MWe	750 MWe

Note: 1 residence equivalent = 100 m².
Source: TMD (2013).

and balneological facilities. While tapping the remaining potential and reaching targets set for 2018 will require an investment of US$5 billion, the constant rise of oil and gas prices is likely to make the investment feasible. In the Turkish context, geothermal energy has proved to be cleaner and much cheaper than fossil fuels. Nevertheless, a number of challenges need to be dealt with to ensure the development and widespread use of this renewable energy source. These include investigating geothermal resources thoroughly, making incentives in district heating more attractive to the private sector and promoting the transfer of expertise.

Acknowledgements

Nilgün Başarır

References

Except where other sources are cited, information in this chapter is adapted from:

Başarır, N. 2013. *Existing Geothermal Situation and Projections in Turkey: Case Study.* Ankara, Turkish Geothermal Association. (Unpublished)

****

Erdoğdu, E. 2009. A snapshot of geothermal energy potential and utilization in Turkey. *Renewable and Sustainable Energy Reviews,* 13(9): 2535–2543.

GEA (Geothermal Energy Association). 2012. *Geothermal: International Market Overview Report.* Washington DC, GEA. http://geo-energy.org/pdf/reports/2012-GEA_International_Overview.pdf

Hürriyet. 2013. Her dört dolarlık ithalatın 1 doları enerjiye. *Hürriyet,* 5 March. http://www.hurriyet.com.tr/ekonomi/22741785.asp (In Turkish)

Lally, M. 2011. *US Companies See Growth Potential in Turkey.* RenewableEnergyWorld.com. http://www.renewableenergyworld.com/rea/news/article/2011/08/u-s-companies-see-growth-potential-in-turkey

Mertoğlu, O. and Başarır, N. 2013. *Significant Progress of Geothermal Development Activities in Turkey: A Success Story.* Paper presented at the European Geothermal Congress, Pisa, Italy, 3–7 June 2013.

MFA (Turkish Ministry of Foreign Affairs). 2013. *Economic Outlook of Turkey.* Ankara, MFA. http://www.mfa.gov.tr/prospects-and-recent-developments-in-the-turkish-economy.en.mfa

Serpen, U., Aksoy, N. and Öngür, T. 2010. *2010 Present Status of Geothermal Energy in Turkey.* Proceedings of the Thirty-Fifth Workshop on Geothermal Reservoir Engineering, Stanford, CA, 1–3 February 2010. http://es.stanford.edu/ERE/pdf/IGAstandard/SGW/2010/serpen.pdf

TMD (Turkish Ministry of Development). 2013. 10. Kalkınma Planı (2014-2018) Madencilik Politikaları Özel İhtisas Komisyonu Enerji Hammaddeleri Grubu Jeotermal Çalışma Alt Grubu Raporu. Ankara, Turkish Ministry Of Development, Geothermal Studies Sub Committee, Mining Policies Special Commission for the 10th National Development Plan. http://www.onuncuplan.gov.tr/oik11/K%20alma%20Belgeleri/Jeotermal%20Raporu%2030.11.pdf (In Turkish)

US DOE (United States Department of Energy). 2013. *Direct Use of Geothermal Energy. Energy Efficiency and Renewable Energy.* Washington DC, Geothermal Technologies Office, US DOE. http://www1.eere.energy.gov/geothermal/directuse.html

US EIA (United States Energy Information Administration). 2013. *Levelized Cost of New Generation Resources in the Annual Energy Outlook 2013. Independent Statistics and Analysis.* Washington DC, US EIA. http://www.eia.gov/forecasts/aeo/er/electricity_generation.cfm

BOXES, TABLES AND FIGURES

BOXES

TABLES

FIGURES

PART 6 DATA AND INDICATORS ANNEX

Data and indicators annex

Compiled by WWAP | Engin Koncagül and Sisira Saddhamangala Withanachchi

INDICATOR 1

Demographic projections

	Population growth rate (%)			Population projection (million)				Urban population (%)			
	2015–2020	2020–2025	2025–2030	2015	2020	2025	2030	2015	2020	2025	2030
Africa	2.36	2.24	2.15	1 166 239	1 312 142	1 467 973	1 634 366	41.1	43.2	45.3	47.7
Asia	0.88	0.72	0.57	4 384 844	4 581 523	4 748 915	4 886 846	47.6	50.5	53.1	55.5
Europe	0.01	-0.07	-0.13	743 123	743 569	741 020	736 364	73.8	74.9	76.1	77.4
LAC	0.98	0.86	0.73	630 089	661 724	690 833	716 671	80.2	81.5	82.5	83.4
North America	0.79	0.74	0.68	361 128	375 724	389 939	403 373	83.1	84.1	85.0	85.8
Oceania	1.33	1.23	1.12	39 359	42 066	44 734	47 317	70.8	70.9	71.1	71.4
World	**1.04**	**0.93**	**0.83**	**7 324 782**	**7 716 749**	**8 083 413**	**8 424 937**	**53.9**	**56.0**	**58.0**	**59.9**

Note: LAC, Latin America and the Caribbean.
Source: WWAP, with data for population growth rate (medium variant) from UNDESA (2013, see specifically http://esa.un.org/wpp/unpp/panel_indicators.htm); for population projection (medium variant) from UNDESA (2013, see specifically http://esa.un.org/wpp/unpp/panel_population.htm) and for urban population (percentage of population residing in urban areas), UNDESA (2012, see specifically http://esa.un.org/unup/CD-ROM/WUP2011-F02-Proportion_Urban.xls).

UNDESA (United Nations Department of Economic and Social Affairs), Population Division. 2012. *World Urbanization Prospects, The 2011 Revision.* New York, UN.
————. 2013. *World Urbanization Prospects, The 2012 Revision.* New York, UN. http://esa.un.org/unpd/wpp/index.htm

INDICATOR 2

Urban and rural populations by development group (1950–2050)

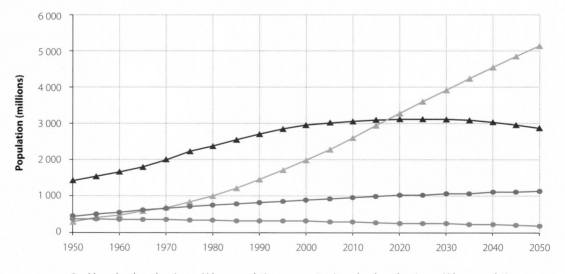

- ● More developed regions – Urban population
- ● More developed regions – Rural population
- ▲ Less developed regions – Urban population
- ▲ Less developed regions – Rural population

Source: UNDESA (2012, fig. 1, p. 3).

UNDESA (United Nations Department of Economic and Social Affairs). 2012. *World Urbanization Prospects, The 2011 Revision: Highlights.* New York, UN. http://esa.un.org/unup/pdf/WUP2011_Highlights.pdf

Total actual renewable water resources per capita (2011)

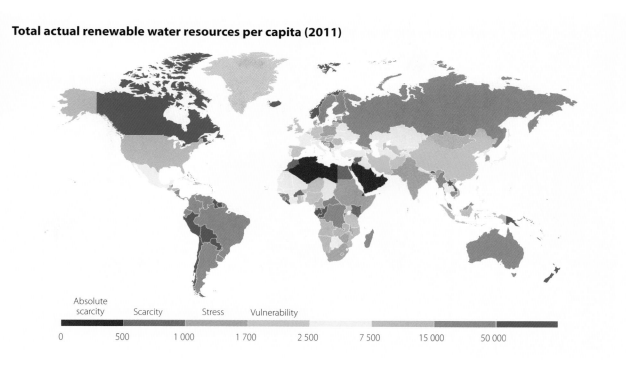

Absolute scarcity   Scarcity   Stress   Vulnerability

| 0 | 500 | 1 000 | 1 700 | 2 500 | 7 500 | 15 000 | 50 000 |

Note: The map shows m³ per capita per year.
Source: WWAP, with data from FAO AQUASTAT database (aggregate data for all countries except Andorra and Serbia, external data) (website accessed Oct 2013), and using UN-Water category thresholds.

Total actual renewable water resources per capita: Trends and projections

	2000	2010	2030	2050
World	**6 936**	**6 148**	**5 095**	**4 556**
Africa	**4 854**	**3 851**	**2 520**	**1 796**
Northern Africa	331	284	226	204
Sub-Saharan Africa	5 812	4 541	2 872	1 983
Americas	**22 930**	**20 480**	**17 347**	**15 976**
Northern America	14 710	13 274	11 318	10 288
Central America and the Caribbean	10 736	9 446	7 566	6 645
Southern America	35 264	31 214	26 556	25 117
Asia	**3 186**	**2 845**	**2 433**	**2 302**
Middle East	1 946	1 588	1 200	1 010
Central Asia	3 089	2 623	1 897	1 529
Southern and Eastern Asia	3 280	2 952	2 563	2 466
Europe	**9 175**	**8 898**	**8 859**	**9 128**
Western and Central Europe	4 258	4 010	3 891	3 929
Eastern Europe	20 497	21 341	22 769	24 874
Oceania	**35 681**	**30 885**	**24 873**	**21 998**
Australia and New Zealand	35 575	30 748	24 832	22 098
Other Pacific Islands	36 920	32 512	25 346	20 941

Source: WWAP, with data from FAO AQUASTAT database (for water resources) (website accessed Dec 2013) and UNDESA (2011) (for population).

UNDESA (United Nations Department of Economic and Social Affairs), Population Division. 2011. *World Urbanization Prospects, The 2010 Revision.* New York, UN.

5

INDICATOR

Annual average monthly blue water scarcity in the world's major river basins (1996–2005)

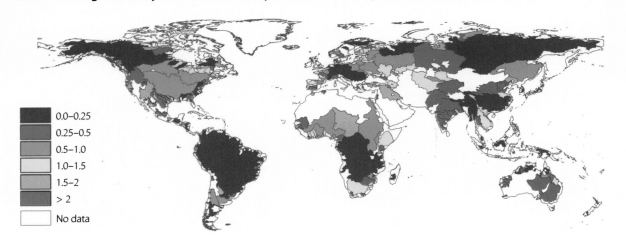

0.0–0.25
0.25–0.5
0.5–1.0
1.0–1.5
1.5–2
> 2
No data

Note: Annual average monthly blue water scarcity in the world's major river basins is calculated by equally weighting the twelve monthly blue water scarcity values per basin.
Source: Hoekstra et al. (2012, fig. 7, p. 23).

Hoekstra, A.Y. and Mekonnen, M.M. 2011. *Global Water Scarcity: Monthly Blue Water Footprint Compared to Blue Water Availability for the World's Major River Basins.* Value of Water Research Report Series No. 53. Delft, The Netherlands, UNESCO-IHE.
http://www.waterfootprint.org/Reports/Report53-GlobalBlueWaterScarcity.pdf

6

INDICATOR

Water withdrawal by sector (around 2006)

	Total withdrawal by sector						Total water withdrawal *	Total water withdrawal per inhabitant	Total water freshwater withdrawal	Freshwater withdrawal as % of IRWR
	Muncipal		Industrial		Agricultural					
	km³/year	%	km³/year	%	km³/year	%	km³/year	m³/year	km³/year	
World	**469**	**12**	**731**	**19**	**2 702**	**69**	**3 902**	**593**	**3 753**	**9**
Africa	**28**	**13**	**11**	**5**	**175**	**82**	**214**	**230**	**202**	**5**
Northern Africa	9	10	6	6	79	84	94	607	82	176
Sub-Saharan Africa	19	16	6	5	95	80	120	155	120	3
Americas	**135**	**16**	**285**	**34**	**409**	**49**	**829**	**927**	**825**	**4**
Northern America	86	14	259	43	259	43	604	1 373	600	10
Central America and the Caribbean	7	23	4	12	20	65	31	390	31	4
Southern America	42	22	22	11	130	67	194	517	194	2
Asia	**228**	**9**	**244**	**10**	**2 035**	**81**	**2 507**	**628**	**2 376**	**20**
Middle East	25	9	20	7	231	84	276	986	268	55
Central Asia	7	5	10	7	128	89	145	1 675	136	56
Southern and Eastern Asia	196	9	214	10	1 676	80	2 086	575	1 973	18
Europe	**72**	**22**	**188**	**57**	**73**	**22**	**333**	**455**	**331**	**5**
Western and Central Europe	53	22	128	54	58	24	239	457	237	11
Eastern Europe	20	21	60	64	15	16	95	450	95	2
Oceania	**5**	**26**	**3**	**15**	**11**	**60**	**18**	**657**	**18**	**2**
Australia and New Zealand	5	26	3	15	11	60	18	710	18	2
Other Pacific Islands	0.03	33	0.01	11	0.05	56	0.1	40	0.1	0.1

Note: * Includes use of desalinated water, direct use of treated municipal wastewater and direct use of agricultural drainage water.
IRWR, internal renewable water resources.
Source: WWAP, with data from FAO AQUASTAT database (accessed Dec 2013).

Water demand at the global level and in country groups (Baseline Scenario 2000 and 2050)

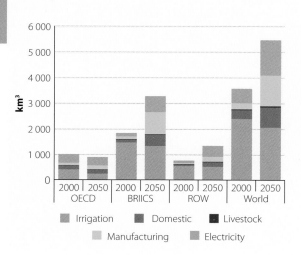

Irrigation
Domestic
Livestock
Manufacturing
Electricity

Note: BRIICS, Brazil, Russia, India, Indonesia, China, South Africa; OECD, Organisation for Economic Co-operation and Development; ROW, rest of the world. This graph only measures 'blue water' demand and does not consider rainfed agriculture.

Source: OECD (2012, fig. 5.4, p. 217, output from IMAGE). *OECD Environmental Outlook to 2050* © OECD.

OECD (Organisation for Economic Co-operation and Development). 2012. *OECD Environmental Outlook to 2050: The Consequences of Inaction*. Paris, OECD. http://dx.doi.org/10.1787/9789264122246-en

Population using solid fuel for cooking and without access to electricity, improved water and sanitation in a selection of countries

	Population (2011)[a] (million)	Electricity (national) Population without access to electricity (2011)[b] (%)	Water (national) Population without access to improved water (2011)[a] (%)	Sanitation (national) Population without access to improved sanitation (2011)[a] (%)	Cooking fuel (national) Population using solid fuel for cooking[*,c] (%)
Africa					
Burkina Faso	17.0	86.9	20.0	82.0	93.0 (2007)
Cameroon	20.0	46.3	25.6	52.2	75.0 (2005)
DR Congo	67.8	91.0	53.8	69.3	95.0 (2007)
Ethiopia	84.7	76.7	51.0	79.3	95.0 (2005)
Ghana	25.0	28.0	13.7	86.5	83.0 (2008)
Kenya	41.6	80.8	39.1	70.6	82.0 (2006)
Malawi	15.4	93.0	16.3	47.1	99.0 (2005)
Nigeria	162.5	52.0	38.9	69.4	75.0 (2007)
Senegal	12.8	43.5	26.6	48.6	56.0 (2006)
South Africa	50.5	15.3	8.5	26.0	17.0 (2007)
Togo	6.2	73.5	41.0	88.6	98.0 (2005)
Uganda	34.5	85.4	25.2	65.0	96.0 (2006)
Asia					
Bangladesh	150.5	40.4	16.8	45.3	91.0 (2007)
Cambodia	14.3	66.0	32.9	66.9	92.0 (2005)
China	1 347.6	0.2	8.3	34.9	55.0 (2000)
India	1 241.5	24.7	8.4	64.9	57.0 (2006)
Indonesia	242.3	27.1	15.7	41.3	55.0 (2007)
Mongolia	2.8	11.8	14.7	47.0	77.0 (2005)
Myanmar	48.3	51.2	15.9	22.7	95.0 (2004)
Nepal	30.5	23.7	12.4	64.6	83.0 (2006)
Pakistan	176.7	31.4	8.6	52.6	67.0 (2006)
Sri Lanka	21.0	14.6	7.4	8.9	78.0 (2006)
Thailand	69.5	1.0	4.2	6.6	34.0 (2005)

Note: * The reference year for the data is given in parentheses. ** Excludes coal.

Source: Compiled by Engin Koncagül and Sisira Saddhamangala Withanachchi (WWAP), with data from [a] WHO/UNICEF (2013, see http://www.wssinfo. org/data-estimates/table/); [b] OECD/IEA (*World Energy Outlook 2013* Electricity Access Database at http://www.worldenergyoutlook.org/media/ weowebsite/energydevelopment/WEO2013Electricitydatabase.xlsx); and [c] WHO Global Health Observatory Data Repository – Solid cooking fuels by country at http://apps.who.int/gho/data/node.main.136?lang=en.

IEA (International Energy Agency). 2012. *World Energy Outlook 2012*. Paris, OECD/IEA.
WHO/UNICEF (World Health Organization/United Nations Children's Fund). 2013. *Data Resources and Estimates*. New York, WHO/UNICEF Joint Monitoring Programme for Water Supply and Sanitation. http://www.wssinfo.org/

	Population (2011)[a] (million)	Electricity (national) Population without access to electricity (2011)[b] (%)	Water (national) Population without access to improved water (2011)[a] (%)	Sanitation (national) Population without access to improved sanitation (2011)[a] (%)	Cooking fuel (national) Population using solid fuel for cooking[*, c] (%)
Latin America					
Argentina	40.8	2.8	0.8	3.7	5.0 (2001)
Bolivia	10.1	13.2	12.0	53.7	29.0 (2007)
Brazil	196.7	0.7	2.8	19.2	13.0 (2003)
Colombia	46.9	2.6	7.1	21.9	15.0 (2005)
Guatemala	14.8	18.1	6.2	19.8	62.0 (2003)
Haiti	10.1	72.1	36.0	73.9	94.0 (2005)
Nicaragua	5.9	22.3	15.0	47.9	57.0 (2006)
Peru	29.4	10.3	14.7	28.4	37.0 (2007)
Middle East					
Iraq	32.7	2.0	15.1	16.1	5.0 (2005)
Syrian Arab Republic	20.8	7.2	10.1	4.8	0.3 (2005)
Yemen	24.8	60.1	45.2	47.0	36.0 (2006)
World	**6 950.7**	**18.1**	**11.1**	**35.9**	**38.0 (2012) ****

Access to improved drinking water (1990–2011)

Region*	Year	Population			Urban Improved			Urban Unimproved	
		x 1 000	Urban (%)	Rural (%)	Total Improved (%)	Piped on premises (%)	Other Improved (%)	Surface water (%)	Total Unimproved (%)
Caucasus and Central Asia	1990	66 627	48.0	52.0	97.0	85.0	12.0	1.0	3.0
	2000	71 294	44.0	56.0	96.0	84.0	12.0	1.0	4.0
	2011	78 177	44.0	56.0	96.0	84.0	12.0	1.0	4.0
Developed countries	1990	1 149 636	72.0	28.0	99.0	97.0	2.0	0.0	1.0
	2000	1 195 732	74.0	26.0	100.0	97.0	3.0	0.0	0.0
	2011	1 249 022	78.0	22.0	100.0	97.0	3.0	0.0	0.0
Eastern Asia	1990	1 216 664	29.0	71.0	97.0	92.0	5.0	1.0	3.0
	2000	1 347 625	38.0	62.0	98.0	93.0	5.0	0.0	2.0
	2011	1 430 886	52.0	48.0	98.0	95.0	3.0	0.0	2.0
Latin America and the Caribbean	1990	443 031	70.0	30.0	94.0	86.0	8.0	1.0	6.0
	2000	521 429	75.0	25.0	96.0	90.0	6.0	1.0	4.0
	2011	596 628	79.0	21.0	97.0	94.0	3.0	0.0	3.0
North Africa	1990	119 693	49.0	51.0	94.0	86.0	8.0	0.0	6.0
	2000	141 978	52.0	48.0	94.0	89.0	5.0	0.0	6.0
	2011	168 355	55.0	45.0	95.0	91.0	4.0	0.0	5.0
Oceania	1990	6 458	24.0	76.0	92.0	74.0	18.0	3.0	8.0
	2000	8 092	24.0	76.0	93.0	75.0	18.0	2.0	7.0
	2011	10 141	23.0	77.0	95.0	74.0	21.0	2.0	5.0
Southern Asia	1990	1 195 984	26.0	74.0	90.0	51.0	39.0	1.0	10.0
	2000	1 460 201	29.0	71.0	92.0	53.0	39.0	1.0	8.0
	2011	1 728 477	33.0	67.0	95.0	54.0	41.0	0.0	5.0
South-East Asia	1990	445 361	32.0	68.0	90.0	41.0	49.0	2.0	10.0
	2000	523 831	38.0	62.0	92.0	45.0	47.0	2.0	8.0
	2011	600 025	45.0	55.0	94.0	51.0	43.0	0.0	6.0
Sub-Saharan Africa	1990	515 587	28.0	72.0	83.0	43.0	40.0	3.0	17.0
	2000	669 117	32.0	68.0	83.0	39.0	44.0	3.0	17.0
	2011	877 563	37.0	63.0	84.0	34.0	50.0	3.0	16.0
Western Asia	1990	127 091	61.0	39.0	95.0	85.0	10.0	1.0	5.0
	2000	161 477	64.0	36.0	96.0	87.0	9.0	1.0	4.0
	2011	211 443	68.0	32.0	96.0	88.0	8.0	0.0	4.0

Note: * Millennium Development Goal (MDG) regions.
Source: WWAP, with data from WHO/UNICEF (2013a, b).

WHO/UNICEF (World Health Organization/United Nations Children's Fund). 2013a. *Progress on Sanitation and Drinking-Water: 2013 Update*. New York, WHO/UNICEF Joint Monitoring Programme for Water Supply and Sanitation.
——. 2013b. *Data Resources and Estimates*. New York, WHO/UNICEF Joint Monitoring Programme for Water Supply and Sanitation.
 http://www.wssinfo.org/data-estimates/table/

Rural Improved		Rural Unimproved		National Improved		National Unimproved		Proportion of the 2011 population that gained access since 1995 (%)
Piped on premises (%)	Total Improved (%)	Surface water (%)	Total Unimproved (%)	Piped on premises (%)	Total Improved (%)	Surface water (%)	Total Unimproved (%)	
31.0	81.0	7.0	18.8	56.0	89.0	4.0	11.0	
29.0	77.0	12.0	23.4	53.0	85.0	7.0	15.0	
29.0	78.0	10.0	21.5	53.0	86.0	6.0	14.0	10
69.0	94.0	0.0	6.3	89.0	98.0	0.0	2.0	
77.0	95.0	0.0	5.0	92.0	98.0	0.0	2.0	
79.0	97.0	1.0	2.8	93.0	99.0	0.0	1.0	7
12.0	56.0	10.0	43.6	35.0	68.0	7.0	32.0	
29.0	71.0	6.0	29.2	53.0	81.0	4.0	19.0	
45.0	85.0	2.0	15.0	71.0	92.0	1.0	8.0	25
38.0	64.0	20.0	36.4	72.0	85.0	7.0	15.0	
50.0	72.0	14.0	27.9	80.0	90.0	4.0	10.0	
64.0	82.0	7.0	18.1	88.0	94.0	2.0	6.0	23
32.0	80.0	3.0	19.9	58.0	87.0	2.0	13.0	
51.0	84.0	4.0	16.2	71.0	89.0	2.0	11.0	
73.0	89.0	5.0	11.4	83.0	92.0	2.0	8.0	23
12.0	36.0	40.0	63.5	27.0	50.0	31.0	50.0	
12.0	41.0	39.0	58.9	27.0	53.0	31.0	47.0	
11.0	45.0	41.0	54.9	25.0	56.0	32.0	44.0	21
7.0	66.0	5.0	33.9	19.0	72.0	4.0	28.0	
11.0	76.0	4.0	23.8	23.0	81.0	3.0	19.0	
15.0	88.0	2.0	12.0	28.0	90.0	1.0	10.0	32
5.0	62.0	12.0	37.9	17.0	71.0	9.0	29.0	
10.0	72.0	9.0	27.9	24.0	80.0	6.0	20.0	
13.0	84.0	3.0	15.7	30.0	89.0	2.0	11.0	28
4.0	35,0	33.0	64.9	15.0	49.0	24.0	51.0	
4.0	42.0	26.0	58.0	15.0	55.0	19.0	45.0	
5.0	51.0	19.0	49.3	15.0	63.0	13.0	37.0	28
41.0	69.0	7.0	30.7	68.0	85.0	3.0	15.0	
53.0	73.0	7.0	26.7	75.0	87.0	3.0	13.0	
66.0	78.0	4.0	21.5	81.0	90.0	1.0	10.0	32

World total primary energy supply by source

(a) 1973

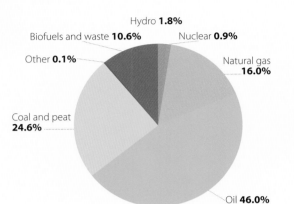

Hydro **1.8%**
Biofuels and waste **10.6%**
Nuclear **0.9%**
Other **0.1%**
Natural gas **16.0%**
Coal and peat **24.6%**
Oil **46.0%**

(b) 2011

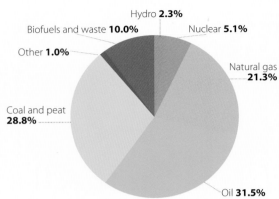

Hydro **2.3%**
Biofuels and waste **10.0%**
Nuclear **5.1%**
Other **1.0%**
Natural gas **21.3%**
Coal and peat **28.8%**
Oil **31.5%**

(a) Fuel share 1973: 6 109 Mtoe total
(b) Fuel share 2011: 13 113 Mtoe total
Note: Mtoe, million tonnes of oil equivalent. 'Other' includes geothermal, solar, wind, heat, etc.
Source: IEA (2013, p. 6, bottom panel). *Key World Energy Statistics 2013* © OECD/IEA.

IEA (International Energy Agency). 2013. *Key World Energy Statistics 2013*. Paris, OECD/IEA.

World primary energy demand: Trends and projections

	2000	2010	New Policies		Current Policies		450 Scenario	
			2020	2035	2020	2035	2020	2035
Total	**10 097**	**12 730**	**14 922**	**17 197**	**15 332**	**18 676**	**14 176**	**14 793**
Coal	2 378	3 474	4 082	4 218	4 417	5 523	3 569	2 337
Oil	3 659	4 113	4 457	4 656	4 542	5 053	4 282	3 682
Gas	2 073	2 740	3 266	4 106	3 341	4 380	3 078	3 293
Nuclear	676	719	898	1 138	886	1 019	939	1 556
Hydro	226	295	388	488	377	460	401	539
Bioenergy*	1 027	1 277	1 532	1 881	1 504	1 741	1 568	2 235
Other renewables	60	112	299	710	265	501	340	1 151
Fossil fuel share in TPED	**80%**	**81%**	**79%**	**75%**	**80%**	**80%**	**77%**	**63%**

Note: All values are in Mtoe unless otherwise noted. * Includes traditional and modern biomass uses. TPED, total primary energy demand.
Source: Adapted from IEA (2012, table 2.1, p. 51).

IEA (International Energy Agency). 2012. *World Energy Outlook 2012*. Paris, OECD/IEA.

Trends in electricity generation in the world and in selected countries (1971–2012)

	1971	1980	1990	2005	2011	2012
Australia	53.3	96.1	155.0	228.7	252.6	252.3
Brazil	51.6	139.4	222.8	403.0	531.8	–
Canada	222.0	373.4	482.2	626.1	637.0	645.8
People's Republic of China	138.4	300.6	621.2	2 502.5	4 715.7	–
France	155.9	258.0	420.7	576.2	562.0	561.2
Germany	329.1	467.6	550.0	620.6	608.7	617.6
India	66.4	119.3	289.4	698.2	1 052.3	–
Japan	385.6	576.3	842.0	1 099.8	1 051.3	1 033.8
Korea	10.5	37.2	105.4	389.4	523.3	531.0
Russian Federation	–	–	1 082.2	953.1	1 054.8	–
United States of America	1 703.4	2 427.3	3 218.6	4 294.4	4 350.0	4 299.8
OECD total	3 847.6	5 684.0	7 672.4	10 575.1	10 867.0	10 833.5
European Union-27	–	–	2 586.3	3 310.6	3 279.2	–
World	**5 256.5**	**8 297.8**	**11 865.7**	**18 335.8**	**22 201.0**	**–**

Note: All figures are in TWh. –, data not available.
Source: WWAP, with data from IEA (2013).

IEA (International Energy Agency). 2013. *World Indicators*. World energy statistics and balances database. Paris, OECD/IEA.
doi: 10.1787/data-00510-en (Accessed Dec 2013)

Trends in world electricity generation by energy source

(a)

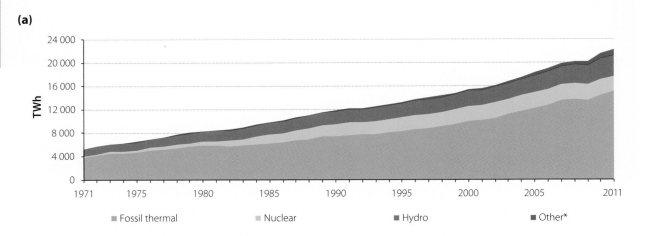

■ Fossil thermal   ■ Nuclear   ■ Hydro   ■ Other*

(b) 1973   **(c) 2011**

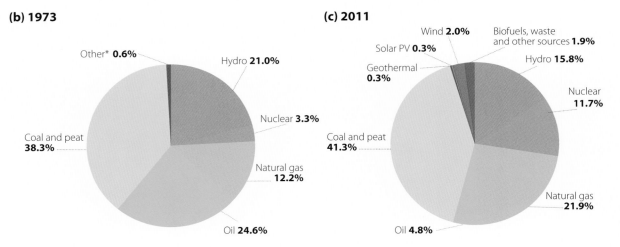

(a) 1971–2011
(b) 1973: 6 115 TWh total
(c) 2011: 22 126 TWh total
Note: Excludes pumped storage. * 'Other' includes geothermal, solar, wind, biofuels and waste, and heat. PV, solar photovoltaic.
Source: IEA (http://www.iea.org/statistics/statisticssearch/report/?&country=WORLD&year=2011&product=ElectricityandHeat) and (2013, p. 24). *Key World Energy Statistics 2013* © OECD/IEA.

IEA (International Energy Agency). 2013. *Key World Energy Statistics 2013*. Paris, OECD/IEA.

Trends in electricity consumption (2000–2011)

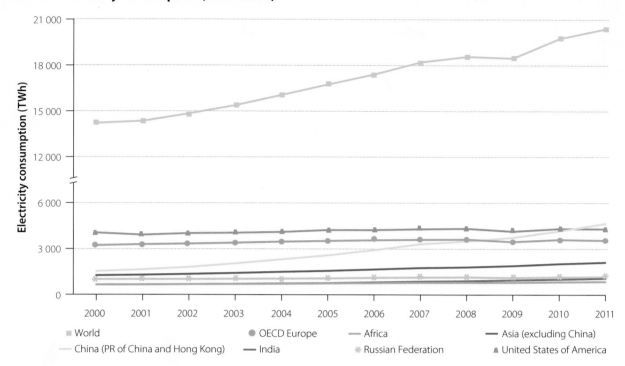

Source: WWAP, with data from IEA (2013).

IEA (International Energy Agency). 2013. *World Indicators*. World energy statistics and balances database. Paris, OECD/IEA. doi: 10.1787/data-00514-en (Accessed Dec 2013)

Share of people without electricity access in developing countries (2011)

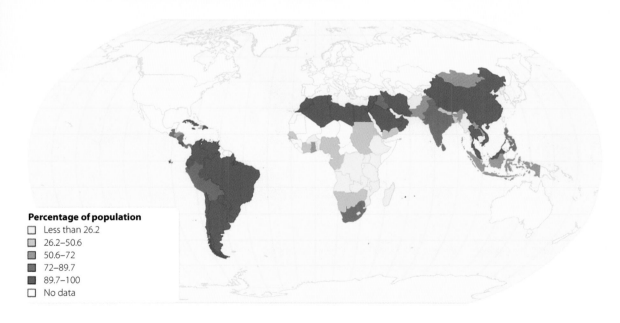

Note: Data are given as a percentage of the population.
Source: ChartsBin.com (http://chartsbin.com/view/10471, based on source cited therein [original data from IEA World Energy Outlook statistics at http://www.iea.org/stats/index.asp]) (Accessed Oct 2013) and updated with data from the IEA *World Energy Outlook 2013* Electricity Access Database (http://www.worldenergyoutlook.org/media/weowebsite/energydevelopment/WEO2013Electricitydatabase.xlsx) for India and Nicaragua.

Global electricity access rate: Trends and projections

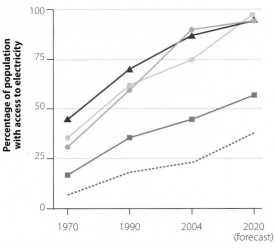

- ▲ Latin America
- ● Mid-East/North Africa
- ● East Asia and Pacific
- ■ South Asia
- ···· Africa

Source: Cosgrove-Davies (2006).

Cosgrove-Davies, M. 2006. *Energy Access in Sub-Saharan Africa – A World Bank Action Plan: Programme Of Action For The Least Developed Countries (2001–2010)*. Presentation, Geneva, 18–19 July 2006. Africa Energy Unit, The World Bank. http://www.unohrlls.org/UserFiles/File/LDC%20 Documents/Workshop/worldbank2006.pdf

Energy consumption per capita (2010)

Note: BTU, British Thermal Unit. One million BTU approximately equals the energy derived from 30 litres of petrol.
Source: Burn: An Energy Journal (http://burnanenergyjournal.com/wp-content/uploads/2013/03/WorldMap_EnergyConsumptionPerCapita2010_v4_BargraphKey.jpg, from sources cited therein) (Accessed Oct 2013). Produced by Anrica Deb for SoundVision Productions®, used with permission.

Trends in electricity consumption per capita (2000–2011)

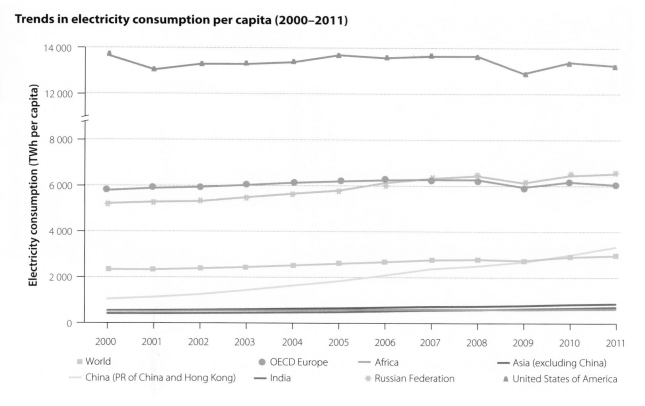

Source: WWAP, with data from IEA (2013).

IEA (International Energy Agency). 2013. *World Indicators*. World energy statistics and balances database. Paris, OECD/IEA. doi: 10.1787/data-00514-en (Accessed Dec 2013)

Use of dams by purpose

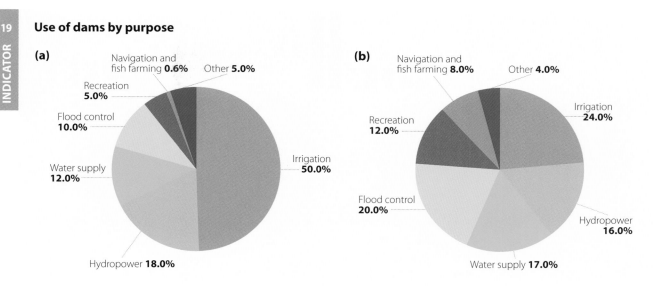

(a) Single purpose dams
(b) Multi purpose dams
Source: WWAP, with data from ICOLD (n.d.).

ICOLD (International Commission on Large Dams). n.d. General Synthesis. Paris, ICOLD.
http://www.icold-cigb.net/GB/World_register/general_synthesis.asp (Accessed Dec 2013)

Total dam capacity per capita by region (around 2010)

Africa

Dam capacity per capita (m³/inhabitant)

8 000
7 000
6 000
5 000
4 000
3 000
2 000
1 000
0

Ethiopia, Namibia, Morocco, South Africa, Mali, Lesotho, Côte d'Ivoire, Egypt, Uganda, Mozambique, Ghana, Zambia, Zimbabwe

Asia

Dam capacity per capita (m³/inhabitant)

6 000
5 000
4 000
3 000
2 000
1 000
0

India, China, Iran (IR), Korea (DPR), Georgia, Thailand, Turkmenistan, Lao (PDR), Turkey, Azerbaijan, Iraq, Kazakhstan

America and Oceania

Dam capacity per capita (m³/inhabitant)

50 000
45 000
40 000
35 000
30 000
25 000
20 000
15 000
10 000
5 000
0

Nicaragua, Peru, Honduras, Mexico, United States of America, Brazil, Australia, New Zealand, Venezuela (BR), Uruguay, Paraguay, Canada, Suriname

Europe

Dam capacity per capita (m³/inhabitant)

8 000
7 000
6 000
5 000
4 000
3 000
2 000
1 000
0

Germany, United Kingdom, France, Czech Republic, Romania, Netherlands, Ukraine, Spain, Albania, Sweden, Russian Federation, Norway

Source: WWAP, with data from FAO AQUASTAT database (accessed Dec 2013).

Hydropower: Technical potential and installed capacity by region (2009)

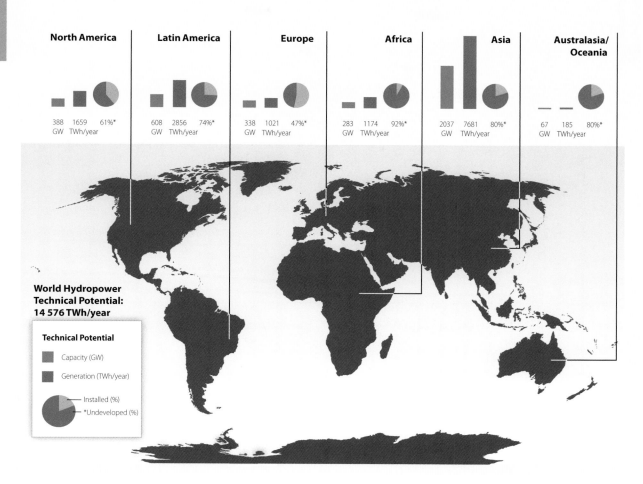

North America	Latin America	Europe	Africa	Asia	Australasia/ Oceania
388 GW 1659 TWh/year 61%*	608 GW 2856 TWh/year 74%*	338 GW 1021 TWh/year 47%*	283 GW 1174 TWh/year 92%*	2037 GW 7681 TWh/year 80%*	67 GW 185 TWh/year 80%*

World Hydropower Technical Potential: 14 576 TWh/year

Technical Potential

- Capacity (GW)
- Generation (TWh/year)
- Installed (%)
- *Undeveloped (%)

Source: Kumar *et al.* (2011, fig. 5.2, p. 445, based on source cited therein). © IPCC.

Kumar, A., Schei, T., Ahenkorah, A., Caceres Rodriguez, R., Devernay, J-M., Freitas, M., Hall, D., Killingtveit, A. and Liu, Z. 2011. Hydropower. O. Edenhofer, R. Pichs-Madruga, Y. Sokona, K. Seyboth, P. Matschoss, S. Kadner, T. Zwickel, P. Eickemeier, G. Hansen, S. Schlomer and C. von Stechow (eds), *IPCC Special Report on Renewable Energy Sources and Climate Change Mitigation.* Cambridge, UK and New York, Cambridge University Press, pp. 437–496.

Trends in hydropower production in selected regions and countries

(a)

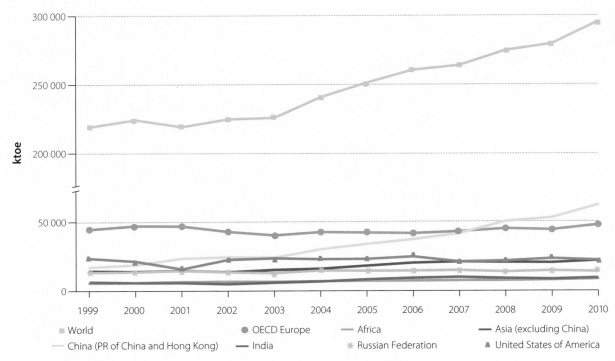

(b) 1973

(c) 2011

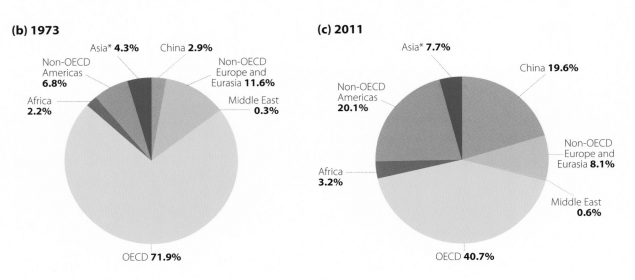

(a) Regional shares 1999–2010

(b) Regional shares 1973: 1 294 TWh total

(c) Regional shares 2011: 3 566 TWh total

Note: Values for (b) and (c) include pumped storage. * Excludes China.

Source: WWAP, with data for (a) from IEA (2013a) and for (b, c) from IEA (2013b, p. 18, bottom panel). *Key World Energy Statistics 2013* © OECD/IEA.

IEA (International Energy Agency). 2013a. *Extended World Energy Balances*. World energy statistics and balances database. Paris, OECD/IEA. doi: 10.1787/data-00513-en (Accessed Dec 2013)

---- 2013b. *Key World Energy Statistics 2013*. Paris, OECD/IEA.

Global water use for energy production by scenario

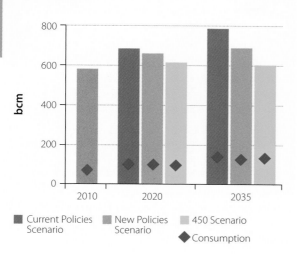

Current Policies Scenario ■
New Policies Scenario ■
450 Scenario ■
◆ Consumption

Source: WWAP, with data from IEA (2012).

IEA (International Energy Agency). 2012. *World Energy Outlook 2012*. Paris, OECD/IEA.

Energy requirement to deliver 1 m³ water safe for human consumption from various water sources

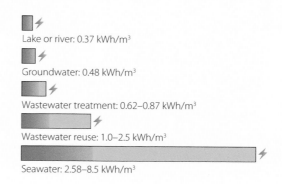

Lake or river: 0.37 kWh/m³

Groundwater: 0.48 kWh/m³

Wastewater treatment: 0.62–0.87 kWh/m³

Wastewater reuse: 1.0–2.5 kWh/m³

Seawater: 2.58–8.5 kWh/m³

Note: This diagram does not incorporate critical elements such as the distance the water is transported or the level of efficiency, which vary greatly from site to site.
Source: WBSCD (2009, fig. 5, p. 14, based on source cited therein).

WBCSD (World Business Council on Sustainable Development). 2009. *Water, Energy and Climate Change: A Contribution from the Business Community*. Geneva, WBCSD. http://www.wbcsd.org/pages/edocument/edocumentdetails.aspx?id=40&nosearchcontextkey=true

Indicative energy use of municipal water and wastewater services

Energy using activity		Indicative share	Comments
Water supply			
Raw water extraction	Pumping Building services	Surface water: 10% Groundwater: 30%	
Treatment	Mixing Other treatment processes Pumping (for backwash etc.) Water sludge processing and disposal Building services	Surface water: 10% Groundwater: 1%	
Clean water transmission and distribution	Pumping	Surface water: 80% Groundwater: 69%	Dependent on the share of gravity-fed water supply
Wastewater management (activated sludge treatment process)			
Wastewater collection	Pumping	10%	Dependent on the share of gravity-induced collection
Treatment	Aeration Other treatment processes Building services	55%	Mostly for aeration of wastewater
Sludge treatment and disposal	Centrifugal and press dewatering Sludge pumping, storing and residue burial Building services	35%	Energy can be produced in sludge processing

Source: World Bank (2012, table 2.1, p. 12). © World Bank, Washington, DC.

World Bank. 2012. *A Primer on Energy Efficiency for Municipal Water and Wastewater Utilities*. Energy Sector Management Assistance Program Technical Report 001/12. Washington DC, World Bank.
http://documents.worldbank.org/curated/en/2012/02/16253058/primer-energy-efficiency-municipal-water-wastewater-utilities

Energy requirements and cost implications of desalination by technology

Technology	Thermal processes		Membrane separation processes	
	Multi stage flash (MSF)	Multi effect distillation (MED)	Reverse osmosis (RO)	Electrodialysis (ED)
Typical total energy use (kWh/m³)	5	2.75	2.5	2.75
Operation temperature (°C)	90–110	70	Room temperature	Room temperature
Market share (%)	27	8	60	4
Capital cost per unit of capacity	USD 800–1,500/m³/day; large variations depending on local labour cost, interest rates and technology			
Freshwater production cost	USD 1–2/m³ (USD 0.5/m³ for large plants); largely dependent on energy cost and plant location			

Note: Desalination requires a considerable amount of energy. The table shows key typical energy data for different desalination technologies. Taking into account the average energy demand of desalination processes, the global desalination capacity (i.e. 65.2 million m³/day) requires the use of approximately 206 million kWh/day, equivalent to 75.2 TWh/year.
Source: Adapted from IEA-ETSAP and IRENA (2012, table 5, p. 21).

IEA-ETSAP and IRENA. 2012. *Water Desalination Using Renewable Energy*. Technology Brief I12. Paris/Abu Dhabi, IRENA/IEA-ETSAP. http://www.irena.org/DocumentDownloads/Publications/IRENA-ETSAP%20Tech%20Brief%20I12%20Water-Desalination.pdf

Global cumulative contracted versus commissioned daily desalination capacity (2013)

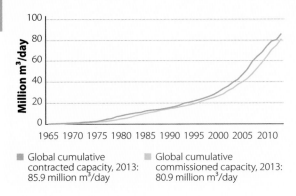

■ Global cumulative contracted capacity, 2013: 85.9 million m³/day   ■ Global cumulative commissioned capacity, 2013: 80.9 million m³/day

Source: Global Water Intelligence/Desaldata.

Power consumption trends in seawater reverse osmosis desalination (1985–2009)

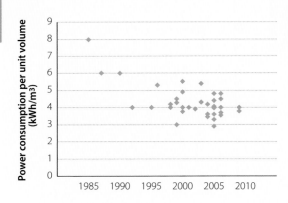

Source: Global Water Intelligence/Desaldata.

Water footprint of energy generation by fuel

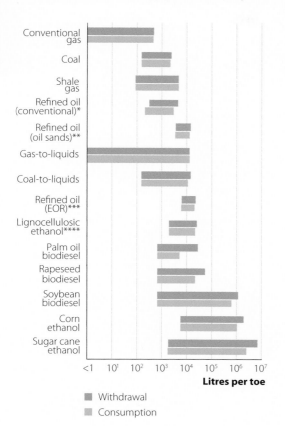

Litres per toe

- ■ Withdrawal
- ■ Consumption

Note: * The minimum is for primary recovery; the maximum is for secondary recovery. ** The minimum is for in-situ production, the maximum is for surface mining. *** Includes carbon dioxide injection, steam injection and alkaline injection and in-situ combustion.
**** Excludes water use for crop residues allocated to food production. toe, tonne of oil equivalent (1 toe = 11.63 MWh = 41.9 GJ). Ranges shown are for 'source-to-carrier' primary energy production, which includes withdrawals and consumption for extraction, processing and transport. Water use for biofuels production varies considerably because of differences in irrigation needs among regions and crops; the minimum for each crop represents non-irrigated crops whose only water requirements are for processing into fuels. EOR, enhanced oil recovery.
For numeric ranges, see http://www.worldenergyoutlook.org.
Source: IEA (2012, fig. 17.3, p. 507, based on sources cited therein). *World Energy Outlook 2012* © OECD/IEA.

IEA (International Energy Agency). 2012. *World Energy Outlook 2012.* Paris, OECD/IEA.

Water use for electricity generation by cooling technology

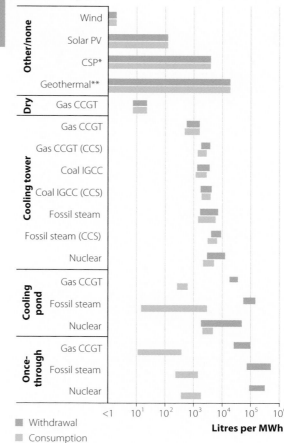

Litres per MWh

- ■ Withdrawal
- ■ Consumption

Note: * Includes trough, tower and Fresnel technologies using tower, dry and hybrid cooling, and Stirling technology. ** Includes binary, flash and enhanced geothermal system technologies using tower, dry and hybrid cooling.
Ranges shown are for the operational phase of electricity generation, which includes cleaning, cooling and other process related needs; water used for the production of input fuels is excluded. Fossil steam includes coal-, gas- and oil-fired power plants operating on a steam cycle. Reported data from power plant operations are used for fossil-steam once-through cooling; other ranges are based on estimates summarized in the sources cited. Solar PV, solar photovoltaic; CSP, concentrating solar power; CCGT, combined-cycle gas turbine; IGCC, integrated gasification combined-cycle; CCS, carbon capture and storage. For numeric ranges, see http://www.worldenergyoutlook.org.
Source: IEA (2012, fig. 17.4, p. 510, from sources cited therein). *World Energy Outlook 2012* © OECD/IEA.

IEA (International Energy Agency). 2012. *World Energy Outlook 2012.* Paris, OECD/IEA.

Trends in ISO 14001 certification (1999–2012)

Overview

Year	1999	2000	2001	2002	2003	2004
Total	**13 994**	**22 847**	**36 464**	**49 440**	**64 996**	**90 554**
Africa	129	228	311	418	626	817
Central and South America	309	556	681	1 418	1 691	2 955
North America	975	1 676	2 700	4 053	5 233	6 743
Europe	7 253	10 971	17 941	23 305	30 918	39 805
East Asia and Pacific	5 120	8 993	14 218	19 307	25 151	38 050
Central and South Asia	114	267	419	636	927	1 322
Middle East	94	156	194	303	450	862

Regional share

Year	1999	2000	2001	2002	2003	2004
Africa	0.9%	1.0%	0.9%	0.8%	1.0%	0.9%
Central and South America	2.2%	2.4%	1.9%	2.9%	2.6%	3.3%
North America	7.0%	7.3%	7.4%	8.2%	8.1%	7.4%
Europe	51.8%	48.0%	49.2%	47.1%	47.6%	44.0%
East Asia and Pacific	36.6%	39.4%	39.0%	39.1%	38.7%	42.0%
Central and South Asia	0.8%	1.2%	1.1%	1.3%	1.4%	1.5%
Middle East	0.7%	0.7%	0.5%	0.6%	0.7%	1.0%

Annual growth: Absolute numbers

Year	2000	2001	2002	2003	2004
Total	**8 853**	**13 617**	**12 976**	**15 556**	**25 558**
Africa	99	83	107	208	191
Central and South America	247	125	737	273	1 264
North America	701	1 024	1 353	1 180	1 510
Europe	3 718	6 970	5 364	7 613	8 887
East Asia and Pacific	3 873	5 225	5 089	5 844	12 899
Central and South Asia	153	152	217	291	395
Middle East	62	38	109	147	412

Source: WWAP, with data from ISO (2012).

ISO (International Organization for Standardization). *ISO Survey 2102*. Geneva, ISO.
http://www.iso.org/iso/home/standards/certification/iso-survey.htm#

2005	2006	2007	2008	2009	2010	2011	2012
111 163	**128 211**	**154 572**	**188 574**	**222 974**	**251 548**	**261 926**	**285 844**
1 130	1 079	1 096	1 518	1 531	1 675	1 740	2 109
3 411	4 355	4 260	4 413	3 748	6 999	7 105	8 202
7 119	7 673	7 267	7 194	7 316	6 302	7 450	8 573
47 837	55 919	65 097	78 118	89 237	103 126	101 177	113 356
48 800	55 428	72 350	91 156	113 850	126 551	137 335	145 724
1 829	2 201	2 926	3 770	4 517	4 380	4 725	4 946
1 037	1 556	1 576	2 405	2 775	2 515	2 425	2 934

2005	2006	2007	2008	2009	2010	2011	2012
1.0%	0.8%	0.7%	0.8%	0.7%	0.7%	0.7%	0.7%
3.1%	3.4%	2.8%	2.3%	1.7%	2.8%	2.7%	2.9%
6.4%	6.0%	4.7%	3.8%	3.3%	2.5%	2.8%	3.0%
43.0%	43.6%	42.1%	41.4%	40.0%	41.0%	38.6%	39.7%
43.9%	43.2%	46.8%	48.3%	51.1%	50.3%	52.4%	51.0%
1.6%	1.7%	1.9%	2.0%	2.0%	1.7%	1.8%	1.7%
0.9%	1.2%	1,0%	1.3%	1.2%	1.0%	0.9%	1.0%

2005	2006	2007	2008	2009	2010	2011	2012
20 609	**17 048**	**26 361**	**34 002**	**34 400**	**28 574**	**10 378**	**23 918**
313	-51	17	422	13	144	65	369
456	944	-95	153	-665	3 251	75	1 128
376	554	-406	-73	122	-1 014	1 148	1 123
8 032	8 082	9 178	13 021	11 119	13 889	-1 949	12 179
10 750	6 628	16 922	18 806	22 694	12 701	10 784	8 389
507	372	725	844	747	-137	345	221
175	519	20	829	370	-260	-90	509

ISO 50001 certification on energy management

Africa

Year	2011	2012
Total	**0**	**13**
Egypt	0	6
Ethiopia	0	1
Malawi	0	1
Mozambique	0	1
South Africa	0	1
Tanzania, UR	0	1
Uganda	0	1
Zambia	0	1

Central and South America

Year	2011	2012
Total	**11**	**7**
Argentina	0	1
Brazil	2	3
Chile	0	3
Grenada	9	0

North America

Year	2011	2012
Total	**1**	**4**
United States of America	1	3
Mexico	0	1

East Asia and Pacific

Year	2011	2012
Total	**49**	**134**
China	0	3
Hong Kong, China	1	4
Macau, China	0	1
Taipei, Chinese	11	37
Japan	8	15
Republic of Korea	19	21
Malaysia	0	2
Philippines	0	1
Singapore	0	4
Thailand	10	41
Viet Nam	0	5

Europe

Year	2011	2012
Total	**364**	**1 758**
Austria	4	29
Belgium	0	16
Bulgaria	0	1
Croatia	0	4
Czech Republic	1	10
Denmark	26	85
Finland	1	6
France	3	35
Germany	42	1 115
Greece	2	9
Hungary	0	2
Ireland	0	35
Italy	30	66
Netherlands	0	15
Norway	9	9
Poland	2	10
Portugal	1	3
Romania	66	54
Russian Federation	1	8
Serbia	0	2
Slovakia	0	1
Slovenia	3	8
Spain	95	120
Sweden	62	72
Switzerland	3	14
The Former Yugoslav Republic of Macedonia	0	2
Turkey	2	1
Ukraine	0	2
United Kingdom	11	24

Source: WWAP, with data from ISO (2012).

ISO (International Organization for Standardization). *ISO Survey 2102*. Geneva, ISO. http://www.iso.org/iso/home/standards/certification/iso-survey.htm#

Middle East

Year	2011	2012
Total	**8**	**18**
Iran, Islamic Republic	0	1
Israel	4	9
Saudi Arabia	0	2
United Arab Emirates	4	6

Central and South Asia

Year	2011	2012
Total	**26**	**47**
India	25	45
Kazakhstan	0	1
Sri Lanka	1	1

Trends in geothermal electricity output (2000–2011)

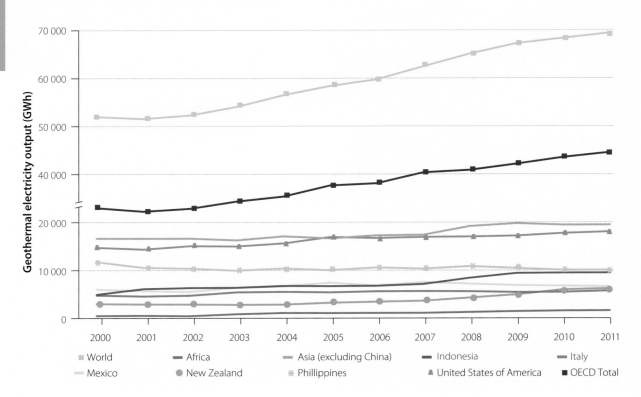

Legend:
- ■ World
- ━ Africa
- ━ Asia (excluding China)
- ━ Indonesia
- ━ Italy
- ━ Mexico
- ● New Zealand
- ✳ Phillippines
- ▲ United States of America
- ■ OECD Total

Source: WWAP, with data from IEA (2013).

IEA (International Energy Agency). 2013a. *World Energy Balances.* World energy statistics and balances database. Paris, OECD/IEA. doi: 10.1787/data-00512-en (Accessed Dec 2013)

Worldwide installed capacity for geothermal electricity generation (2010)

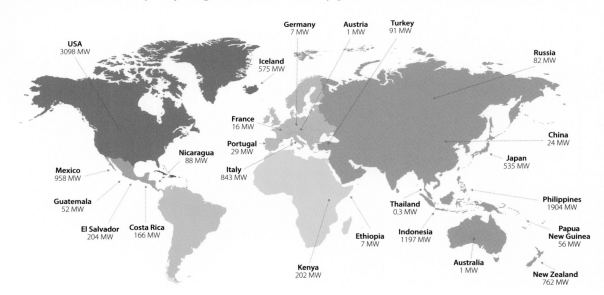

- Germany 7 MW
- Austria 1 MW
- Turkey 91 MW
- USA 3098 MW
- Iceland 575 MW
- Russia 82 MW
- France 16 MW
- Portugal 29 MW
- China 24 MW
- Nicaragua 88 MW
- Italy 843 MW
- Japan 535 MW
- Mexico 958 MW
- Philippines 1904 MW
- Guatemala 52 MW
- Thailand 0.3 MW
- Papua New Guinea 56 MW
- El Salvador 204 MW
- Costa Rica 166 MW
- Ethiopia 7 MW
- Indonesia 1197 MW
- Australia 1 MW
- Kenya 202 MW
- New Zealand 762 MW

Note: Worldwide total: 10.9 GW.
Source: Bertani (2012, fig. 2, p. 3).

Bertani, R. 2012. Geothermal Power Generation in the World, 2005–2010 Update Report. *Geothermics*, 41: 1–29.

Global trends in ethanol and biodiesel production (1975–2010)

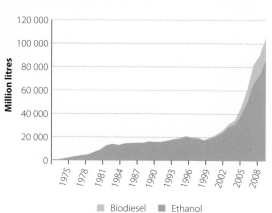

Biodiesel   Ethanol

Source: Shrank and Farahmand (2011, fig. 1, from source cited therein).

Shrank, S. and Farahmand, F. 2011. Biofuels regain momentum. *Vital Signs Online*, 29 August. Washington DC, WorldWatch Institute. http://vitalsigns.worldwatch.org/vs-trend/biofuels-regain-momentum

Indicative yields and water requirements for some major biofuel crops

Crop	Fuel product	Annual obtainable yield (L/ha)	Energy yield (GJ/ha)	Potential crop evapo-transpiration (in mm, indicative)	Evapo-transpiration (L/L fuel)	Irrigated or rainfed production	Rainfed conditions	Water resource implications under irrigated conditions (assuming an irrigation efficiency of 50%)		
							Actual rainfed crop evapotrans-piration (in mm, indicative)	Irrigation water used (in mm, indicative)	Irrigation water used (in L/L fuel, indicative)
Sugar-cane	Ethanol (from sugar)	6 000	120	1 400	2 000	Irrigated/ rainfed	1 100	600	1 000
Sugar beet	Ethanol (from sugar)	7 000	140	650	786	Irrigated/ rainfed	450	400	571
Cassava	Ethanol (from starch)	4 000	80	1 000	2 250	Rainfed	900	–	–
Maize	Ethanol (from starch)	3 500	70	550	1 360	Irrigated/ rainfed	400	300	857
Winter wheat	Ethanol (from starch)	2 000	40	300	1 500	Rainfed	300	–	–
Palm oil	Bio-diesel	6 000	193	1 500	2 360	Rainfed	1 300	–	–
Rapeseed/ mustard	Bio-diesel	1 200	42	500	3 330	Rainfed	400	–	–
Soybean	Bio-diesel	450	14	500	10 000	Rainfed	400	–	–

Note: 1 GJ/h = 277.8 kW.
Source: Hoogeveen *et al.* (2009, table II, p. S153, adapted from source cited therein).

Hoogeveen, J., Faurès, J-M. and van de Giessen, N. 2009. Increased biofuel production in the coming decade: To what extent will it affect global freshwater resources? *Irrigation and Drainage*, doi:10.1002/ird.479

37
INDICATOR

Global total final energy consumption versus share of renewable energy

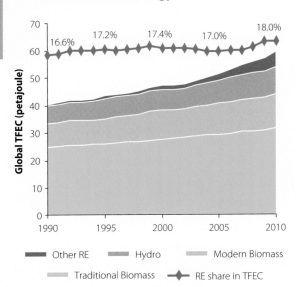

Note: RE, renewable energy; TFEC, total final energy consumption.
Source: Banerjee et al. (2013, fig. 4.5, p. 209, based on IEA data cited therein).
© World Bank, Washington, DC.

Banerjee, S.G., Bhatia, M., Azuela, G.E., Jaques, I., Sarkar, A., Portale, E., Bushueva, I., Angelou, N. and Inon, J.G. 2013. *Global tracking framework. Global Tracking Framework, Vol. 3. Sustainable Energy for All.* Washington DC, The World Bank. http://documents.worldbank.org/curated/en/2013/05/17765643/global-tracking-framework-vol-3-3-main-report

38
INDICATOR

The importance of water for energy

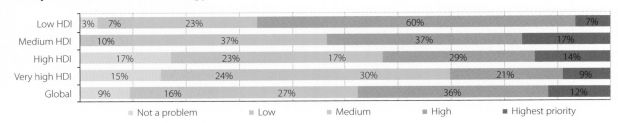

Note: The indicator shows the current status in responding countries by Human Development Index (HDI) groups.
Source: UNEP (2012, fig. 8.9, p. 65).

UNEP (United Nations Environment Programme). 2012. *The UN-Water Status Report on the Application of Integrated Approaches to Water Resources Management.* Nairobi, UNEP. http://www.un.org/waterforlifedecade/pdf/un_water_status_report_2012.pdf

39
INDICATOR

Perceived change over the past 20 years in the importance of water for energy

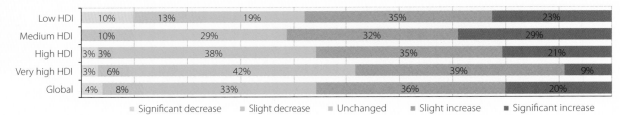

Note: The indicator shows current status in responding countries by Human Development Index (HDI) groups.
Source: UNEP (2012, fig. 8.10, p. 65).

UNEP (United Nations Environment Programme). 2012. *The UN-Water Status Report on the Application of Integrated Approaches to Water Resources Management.* Nairobi, UNEP. http://www.un.org/waterforlifedecade/pdf/un_water_status_report_2012.pdf

National energy policy/strategy/plan with water resources management component

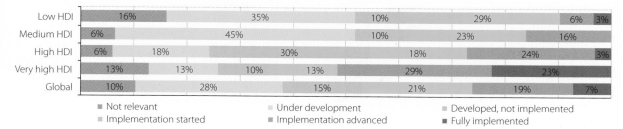

Not relevant • Under development • Developed, not implemented
Implementation started • Implementation advanced • Fully implemented

Note: The indicator shows the current status in responding countries by Human Development Index (HDI) groups.
Source: UNEP (2012, fig. 8.11, p. 65).

UNEP (United Nations Environment Programme). 2012. *The UN-Water Status Report on the Application of Integrated Approaches to Water Resources Management.* Nairobi, UNEP. http://www.un.org/waterforlifedecade/pdf/un_water_status_report_2012.pdf

Infrastructure development and mobilizing financing for energy/hydropower

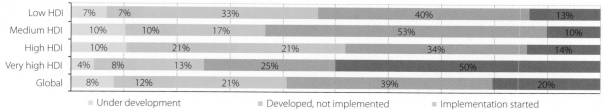

Under development • Developed, not implemented • Implementation started
Implementation advanced • Fully implemented

Note: The indicator shows the current status in responding countries by Human Development Index (HDI) groups.
Source: UNEP (2012, fig. 8.12, p. 65).

UNEP (United Nations Environment Programme). 2012. *The UN-Water Status Report on the Application of Integrated Approaches to Water Resources Management.* Nairobi, UNEP. http://www.un.org/waterforlifedecade/pdf/un_water_status_report_2012.pdf

PHOTO CREDITS